Praise for The Power of Paradox

"The best strategic insights don't always come through linear thinking. Deborah Schroeder-Saulnier makes a great contribution with her approach."

—Greig Woodring, president and Chief Executive Officer, Reinsurance Group of America, Incorporated

"Deborah Schroeder-Saulnier has taken ancient and contemporary wisdom about interdependent pairs (paradox, polarity, dilemma, tensions) and added her own thinking and experience to the mix. The result is a sound, practical book for those wanting to maximize and sustain their organization's potential."

—Barry Johnson, author of Polarity Management; founder, Polarity Partnerships LLC.

"Change your thinking and you change the game in a POWERFUL way! Whether in business or personal life, Deborah Schroeder-Saulnier shows us how 'AND' is often better than 'OR'."

—Jim Myers (aka George "The Animal" Steele)

DEBORAH SCHROEDER-SAULNIER

THE
POWER
OF
PARADOX

Harness the Energy of
Competing Ideas to
Uncover Radically
Innovative Solutions

CAREER
PRESS

Pompton Plains, N.J.

THE POWER OF PARADOX
EDITED BY JODI BRANDON
TYPESET BY EILEEN MUNSON
Cover design by Howard Grossman
Printed in the U.S.A.

To order this title, please call toll-free 1-800-CAREER-1 (NJ and Canada: 201-848-0310) to order using VISA or MasterCard, or for further information on books from Career Press.

CAREER
PRESS

The Career Press, Inc.
220 West Parkway, Unit 12
Pompton Plains, NJ 07444
www.careerpress.com

Library of Congress Cataloging-in-Publication Data
CIP Data Available Upon Request

Acknowledgments

During my career of 25 years in leadership and consulting roles, I have concentrated my energies and a passion for excellence on the growth and improvement of organizations and the people who work within them. I have been quite aware of the many tensions or conflicting pulls (i.e., decentralized and centralized, local and global, task and relationship, sales and operations, etc.) which cause frustration throughout organizations. I have seen leaders take on a problem-solving mindset with a resulting pendulum-effect, as one leader pulls to their side or interest then ultimately is pulled to the other side or interest. Although I was keenly aware of these paradoxes as I grew from childhood into adulthood, it wasn't until I was exposed to the systems thinking of the late Russ Ackoff in the mid-'90s, and then meeting Barry Johnson, founder of Polarity Partnerships, in 2002, that I had language to make sense of this phenomena—the phenomena of interdependent pairs. As a result of this exposure and the deeper learning with the broader polarity community, the value I bring to organizations has been strengthened. In writing this book, I now become a bridge between both communities: polarity and paradox.

I would particularly like to thank the following colleagues who challenged and supported me through a two-year Polarity Mastery program: Beena Sharma, Jake Jacobs, Elaine Yarborough, Allison Conte, Brian Emerson, Laurie Levknecht, Leslie DePol, Michael Rawlings, Patrick Masterson, Kathy Anderson, Peter Dupre, Cherie Woodbury, Cliff Kayser and Clare Dus, and especially Margaret Seidler for giving me the nudge to get the book going!

Countless insights have come from working directly with a wide variety industries and organizations across the world. I would like to give special thanks to the many leaders and client organizations that contributed to the book their real stories to help advance paradox thinking in others: Greig Woodring, CEO, Reinsurance Group of America; Jim Kavanaugh, CEO, World Wide Technology; Ron Levy, former CEO, SSM Health Care-St. Louis Network; Harlan Kent, CEO, Yankee Candle; Pamela Perlmutter, director of development and public relations, Paraquad; Kerry Weiner, MD, chief medical officer, Jerry Wilborn, MD, FCCP, and Rene Toledo, executive director Chicago Region–IPC The Hospitalist Company. Thank you, also, to the many leaders and client organizations that chose to be disguised in the book in order to protect confidentiality.

Sincere thanks goes to my former colleagues in the Clarion Group who directly contributed to this book: Bill McKendree, Chuck Andrew, John Helmkamp, Jon Wheeler, Roy Maurer, Wendy Brown Helmkamp, Darcy Topper, Kim Camire, Liz Mancini. A special thanks to Michelle Turnbull for her development of the models.

I benefited from the learning laboratories provided by previous employers: John Sexton & Company, Oakland Park Inn, Boeing, Hussmann, Ingersoll Rand, Right Management, and for exceptional work with colleagues in St. Louis and around the world. Special thanks to Jim Appleton and Chris Pierce-Cooke, executives who took special interest in "both/and" thinking and applied it early on.

I appreciate the support of Ward Klein, CEO, Energizer; Lori Jacob, CEO, Junior Achievement of Greater St. Louis; and Jim Myers, aka George "The Animal" Steele, Scottrade and Ameren. And thank you to Chris Chadwick, who enabled me to bring paradox thinking to groups of leaders throughout the St. Louis community during Leadership St. Louis, a Focus St. Louis program; and to a group of adults at Living Lord Lutheran Church who embraced paradox thinking "law" and "grace" once exposed to the phenomena of "and."

My academic debts are large: Dr. Robert T. Anderson and the late Dr. Herbert Jackson, professors at Michigan State University; the late

Dr. Glenn White, professor at the University of Missouri, St. Louis; Dr. Jeff Haldeman, professor and doctoral dissertation committee chair at Webster University; Warren Bennis; John Gardner; Edgar Schein; Jay Galbraith; Jim Collins; Ram Charan; Carl Rogers; Gestalt principles; work of Daniel Denison; John Kotter; and Ned Herrmann.

I am particularly fortunate to have Kathy Pennell Cooperman as a colleague and a friend. We have "been there" for each other over these last 25 years—no matter what!

And special thanks to Michael Xu, a dear friend in China whose perspective validated the need for this thinking across Eastern countries, not just the Western world.

Of course, books don't just happen in a vacuum. They have to make their way through a work life full of other commitments. My deepest gratitude to the team at Career Press: Ron Fry, Michael Pye, Laurie Kelly-Pye, Jeff Piasky, Kirsten Dalley, and Jodi Brandon.

And a very special thank you to my agent, Maryann Karinch, who has been a joy to work with. We have experienced many examples of paradox throughout the process of writing this book: needing to balance activity and rest, work and play, structure and flexibility. It has been a great journey and I have learned much. Thank you, Maryann.

Finally, work itself is only a part of a much larger life, in my case one shaped by my family, my children—immediate and extended—whom I love very much! My daughters, Tiffany and Brittany, provide me with love and laughter on a daily basis. My husband, Tom, has been by my side all the way, as my sounding board and my best friend. My mother and father have been inspirational to me. Both have taught me excellence and humility—Mom, an exceptional artist, and Dad, a powerful pastor. I am truly blessed!

Contents

Author's Notes
How Paradox Thinking Is Natural *and* Learned
13

Introduction
17

PART I
THE PROCESS: UNLEASHING THE POWER OF PARADOX

Chapter 1
Paradox Thinking: What Is it and Why Use It?
23

Chapter 2
The ABCs of Using Paradox Thinking
43

Chapter 3
Identifying Paradoxes in Any Organization
73

Chapter 4
The Importance of Leaders at All Levels
99

PART II
IMPLEMENTING THE PROCESS

Chapter 5
Building the Model
123

Chapter 6
Developing Action Steps
139

Chapter 7
Identifying and Using Metrics to Stay on Target
161

Chapter 8
Respecting Context and Complexity
179

PART III
RESULTS OF IMPLEMENTING THE PROCESS

Chapter 9
Going Operational
199

Chapter 10
Success (and Failure) Stories
213

Conclusion
233

Appendix
How-to Summary
239

Chapter Notes
243

Index
249

About the Author
255

How Paradox Thinking
Is Natural and Learned

I have thought in terms of opposites and contradictions much of my life. I had an authoritarian father (powerful pastor) and a permissive mother (exceptional artist), and even as a young child, I saw stark differences in how they parented. I recall choosing selectively what I would take from each: I'll take this from my mom *and* that from my dad. So a both/and approach to issues, challenges, and opportunities was a natural part of my life for as long as I could remember. Much later, my predisposition toward thinking "and" became part of an intentional skill set that I have used to help organizations of all sizes avert disasters and exploit opportunities.

My first academic and professional foray into paradox thinking was guided by Russell L. Ackoff, who introduced me to systems thinking. Russ was a remarkable man who went from a degree in architecture, to a doctorate in philosophy of science, to a senior faculty position at the Wharton School of the University of Pennsylvania, where he not only taught systems sciences and management science, but was also a pioneer in those disciplines. He showed me the value of thinking about the relationship of the part and the whole. He also made the practical application of systems thinking clear to me. This quote, taken from his paper "Science in the Systems Age," sums up the central lesson I learned from him: "A system is more than the sum of its parts; it is an indivisible whole. It loses its essential properties when it is taken apart. The elements of a system may themselves be systems, and every system may be part of a larger system."[1] In short, from Russ I learned principles of how people, structures, and processes work together to create either a healthy or an unhealthy organization. I developed a central focus on cyclical relationships, in addition to cause and effect. I routinely rely on this focus as I show people the value of paradox in the context of business.

At lunch one day, Russ put a glass, a toothpick, a fork, and a spoon in front of him. He created a balanced configuration of the intertwined fork and spoon on the glass by using the toothpick. His architecture background was showing, and the philosopher-systems thinker was also at work (and play). The way the utensils were balanced made them a stable system. (The center of mass of the spoon-fork combination is at the rim of the glass. Any object can be supported at its center of mass.)

If your thinking about your business is truly balanced as you approach issues, challenges, and opportunities, you will have only minor setbacks from time to time. Stay balanced, and it generally doesn't matter what is going on around you. Your model will remain steady _and_ adapt to necessary changes in the future.

Years later, I met Barry Johnson. Seeing what Barry did infused my appreciation for paradox with language, models, and a practical way to help organizations use an understanding of paradox to their bottom-line advantage—to turn around negative financial and personnel situations and put themselves on a track to sustainability.

I facilitated a year-long strategic leadership process for one of my client companies, and Barry was brought in as one of the speakers. The leaders experienced a dramatic shift in thinking and behavior as they became familiar with the concept of *polarity* (Barry's word for what I term *paradox*) and came to focus on the relationship of interdependent pairs in the operation of their business. Armed with new thinking and practical approach, conflicts became opportunities for conversation. Struggles turned into invitations for collaboration. Adversarial relationships became friendships. The seemingly impossible became possible.

Seeing the results for myself, and having the knowledge of these processes in my toolkit, I decided that my dissertation for my doctor of management degree would center on polarity principles. In addition, with a limited number of other candidates, I went through a two-year mastery program to explore and evolve with Barry and others the concept of polarity management/thinking. Another way of expressing that concept is both/and thinking, which is contrasted with seeing one option as better than another.

I want to share a portion of the mission statement of Polarity Partnerships, an organization founded by Barry, so that you have exposure to the greater purpose of what you will learn in this book. My focus is aligned with this mission as well. My career application of it is, and has consistently been, the practical use of leveraging and managing paradoxes in a business environment. The inspiration for the approach, models, and thinking that are covered in the book comes from a more broadly transformational goal, as captured in the Polarity Partnerships' mission statement: "Enhance our quality of life on the planet through

Polarity Thinking." The mission statement concludes with a list of the key benefits of using polarity thinking:

"Achieve your preferred future faster and sustain success

Convert polarized conflicts into synergistic opportunities, and

Increase your ability to thrive in a world of increasing complexity and interdependence"[2]

This statement of benefits serves as a reminder to me that goals can be lofty and practical. I hope this book engenders an appreciation for your ability to grasp the interdependent opposite of whatever comes naturally to you, and put both of them to work for you.

Not only do I intend that this book bring new energy, but I also hope it brings a shift in thinking that helps you see the world anew—both in your business life and in all of your life.

In introducing people to the concept of "and," I often use a quote from futurist Joel Barker that I internalized when I first heard it: "Vision without action is just a dream. Action without vision just passes the time. Vision with action changes the world." His words embody the approach to pairing concepts and objectives that runs throughout this book.

Introduction

Paradox is in the news. Often it *is* the news. It is in all of life; it impacts all of life. It knows no boundaries—geographically, socially, economically, politically, culturally, and organizationally. In this book, I'll share with you how individuals, teams, and organizations can accomplish great things—increased profits to improved personal relationships—by managing paradoxes well.

To start, here is how media are featuring examples of paradox—that is, "and" thinking rather than "versus" thinking:

▶ An MSN Autos article from August 2013, began with the following:

"It's counterintuitive: You can drop the hammer on your all-new 2014 Corvette Stingray, burning rubber to the next stoplight, but then get 29 mpg as you calmly cruise down the highway—that's right, 29 mpg. As engines get smaller and more efficient—yet, paradoxically, more powerful—car buyers are seeking new rides that tickle the adrenal gland without guzzling fuel."[1]

Author Evan Griffey continued his assertion that "versus" was *over*. "And" rules the day; he next described the Porsche 911—as well as 21 other cars that fit the same, basic description: "The Porsche 911 is as iconic as they come, and a serious double-take is in order when you realize that the mighty 400-horsepower Carrera S returns 28 mpg highway.... This 50-year-old has never been better."[2]

"Never been better" means that Porsche (and the other man-ufacturers noted in the article) succeeded in delivering a con-summate paradox in terms of cars; it is, in fact, the Holy Grail of auto manufacturing in terms of modern society's desire for getting somewhere fast with the least possible damage to the environment: muscle _and_ mileage.

▸ The French Paradox Diet involves more animal fat per day than many North American diets and is linked to a reduced risk of cardiovascular disease rather than an increased one: high fat _and_ healthy. The French lifestyle and attitude toward food make a paradox a reality—that is, the management of portions and time devoted to eating differs from that of the typical North American.

▸ _Forging Healthy Connections_, a book released in late 2013, opens with "thoughts to keep in mind as you read this book." The book is about why human beings require close relationships for health and healing and how to develop and strengthen those relationships. Each of these five thoughts contains a set of opposites, both of which are important, interdependent elements in achieving health and healing:

  ▸ Medicine is a left-brained discipline; healing is a right-brained process.

  ▸ Healthy habits come from choices; physical well-being comes from feelings.

  ▸ Stress is vital to self-defense; stress is lethal to health and healing.

  ▸ Autonomy is vital for a human being; vulnerability is vital to connecting with another human being.[3]

These three examples address how people achieve the "impossible" by striving for goals that don't seem as though they belong together—they don't seem compatible. Yet at some point, people started asking "What if...?" and their concurrent pursuit of two, seemingly disparate goals began in earnest. Yes, I could have a muscle car that got decent mileage, and I could eat _foie gras_ and still have a healthy heart. Yes, I could (and should) be both logical and emotional when it comes to my health and well-being. Leveraging and managing such paradoxes is a powerful skill that yields bottom-line advantages in all kinds of professional and personal ways.

This approach runs counter to the "versus" thinking that many of people in Western societies grew up with. According to creativity guru Roger von Oech, the source of our desire to analyze options in terms of "*either* this *or* that" is an integral part of Western education. Von Oech is the founder of the "Innovation in Industry" conferences that lured such entrepreneurs as Steve Jobs, Bill Gates, and Charles Schwab. In his 1983 book, *A Whack on the Side of the Head: How You Can Be More Creative*, he asserted that our formal education system is geared toward teaching people "the one right answer." From childhood to adulthood, many people automatically take on a similar problem-solving mindset as questions and issues arise at home or work.

It has only been since the latter part of the 20th century that paradoxes—or as some say, "polarities"—have been explicitly identified by business and industry members as an important dimension in organizational behavior. Tapping this dimension is not only useful in achieving competitive advantage in business, but also essential in doing so.

In developing my doctoral dissertation on the paradox approach to tackling key business issues, I interviewed a number of people in a variety of professions. The concept of "and" thinking resonated for them because they were seekers:

- Looking for language to fit a current way of thinking.
- Searching for a new way of thinking to address inherent tensions where current ways of thinking was were not working.
- Frustrated by leadership challenges.
- Looking for a new tool for a consultant's toolbox.

Adopting an appreciation for paradox means you no longer have to view conflicting needs separately and address only one rather the other. Paradox thinking unravels the assumption that, if you analyze a situation thoroughly, one option will trump another as the solution of a problem.

Companies do not reach their potential when the modus operandi is either/or decision-making; neither do individuals. When organizations adopt that approach, their profit, morale, and ability to innovate suffer. John Kenneth Galbraith expressed the propensity for either/or thinking as follows: "Faced with the choice between changing one's mind and proving that there is no need to do so, almost everyone gets busy on the proof."[4]

This book offers practical reasons to change your thinking, the tools to support the change, and stories vividly illustrating the value of the change.

PART I

The Process:
Unleashing the Power of Paradox

Chapter 1

Paradox Thinking:
What Is It and Why Use It?

> "The test of a first-rate intelligence is
> the ability to hold two opposed ideas
> in the mind at the same time, and still
> retain the ability to function."
> —F. Scott Fitzgerald, *The Crack-Up*

My new client had a lot on the line. It was no longer the golden years in which companies like his could hold on to the status quo and make profits. Money was tight, and he was feeling intense pressure to make changes that would boost profits immediately.

He started our first meeting with a story I'd heard many times before: "We're struggling. We need to cut costs, but if we don't invest in growth opportunities, the company will wither away."

"Let's look at the challenge through a different lens," I suggested. "There's no law that says you have to cut costs *or* invest in growth, is there?"

He laughed, "Maybe a law of business."

I told him a law like that was meant to be broken. And then I wrote the words "cut costs" on the left side of a paper and "invest in growth" on the right side. Between them, I wrote the word "and."

Cut costs *and* invest in growth.

"How is that possible?" he wondered.

"We're about to figure that out!"

Welcome to paradox thinking.

Definition and Benefits

Paradox thinking is "and" thinking. It is thinking that identifies pairs of opposites and determines how they are interdependent relative to a key goal. In the previous example, the pair of opposites is "cut costs _and_ invest in growth." They are interdependent because both are vital in achieving the goal of a thriving organization. Failure to manage the pair of opposites may result in the company going out of business; at the very least, it will result in its slow decline.

Paradox thinking enables balanced management of conflicting objectives. A company wants to be known for innovation at the same time customers embrace it for its stability, to thrill shareholders with strong short-term revenue results and concurrently take actions to ensure long-term health. From those two examples alone, it should be easy to see how failure to manage a critical pair of opposites results in the company stumbling and, perhaps, failing.

Adopting an appreciation for paradox ends the practice of viewing conflicting needs separately and addressing one over the other. Paradox thinking unravels the assumption that, if we analyze a situation thoroughly, one option will trump another in terms of problem-solving. Organizations do not reach their potential when they habitually use that kind of either/or approach to challenges. Their profit, morale, and ability to innovate suffer. Renowned playwright George Bernard Shaw addressed what it takes to make progress when he said, "The reasonable man adapts himself to the world; the unreasonable one persists in trying to adapt the world to himself. Therefore, all progress depends on the unreasonable man."[1]

Paradox thinking supplements the type of thinking many consider natural. So if you are a linear thinker, for example, you won't stop being a linear thinker and suddenly transform into a complete paradox thinker by reading this book. A linear thinker might look at the challenge of employee performance management like this: "First I will point out the employee's shortfalls, and then I will praise him for his accomplishments." The solution to the employee management problem is a step-by-step progression involving critique *and* reward—but the linear thinker wouldn't necessarily see critique and reward as a pair of interdependent opposites.

To that linear pattern, therefore, paradox thinking adds another way of looking at options and goals. It means looking at the divergent needs for critique *and* reward as linked and necessary in pursuing the goal of *effective* performance management. In other words, paradox thinking adds a level of understanding of the challenge, the ways to address it, and what the intended outcome is. In this example, once the linear thinker makes the connection between critique and reward, and consciously manages both to help the employee improve performance, he establishes an environment for faster behavior change and helps employees hit higher performance levels.

When paradox thinking becomes part of your problem-solving strategy, it has another benefit. It alerts you to when you are over-focusing on one part of the pair at the neglect of the other. That is, it helps your management of issues and actions stay balanced. In the performance management situation, it's possible that you may want focus on the reward more than the critique, of course. Doing that deliberately and keeping in touch with the outcomes of that action will help you in the future. But if you are unaware of that emphasis on reward over critique, then you may have just created a problem for yourself.

Paradox in the Language of Business

Many business-related concepts suggest opposing needs. For example, customer service implies the "push" of providing something to customers and the "pull" of finding out what the customer wants. Contract negotiation entails dual requirements: to listen/pay attention *and* talk/demand attention. More than any others, however, two elements stand out as embodying multiple, significant paradoxes: innovation and leadership.

In a business context, innovations tend to involve imagination *and* logic, a focus on what's different *and* what's familiar, being practical *and* stretching for the incredible, and many more interdependent opposites. Michael S. Dobson, author of *Creative Project Management* among other engaging business books, told me this story of innovation from early in his career:

> I was at the toy fair with my boss, looking around the show floor for the next big thing. This was the year the Cabbage Patch Kids became a fad. We were in some Hong Kong importer's show room and they were selling Broccoli Patch Kids. They were a terrible knockoff. I made some disparaging remarks about them and my boss said, "You have to understand that it's not bad that it's a knockoff. It's just a dumb knockoff. There is a brilliant Cabbage Patch knockoff at this show. See if you can find it."
>
> I looked around for hours and didn't see anything that fit his description. At the end of the day, he said, "What is the Cabbage Patch gimmick?"
>
> That much I knew: "You adopt them."
>
> "What else do you adopt?"
>
> That was a gigantic clue. The brilliant Cabbage Patch knockoff at that year's toy fair was Pound Puppies. They are exactly like Cabbage Patch dolls, but completely different.

The ideal toy is brand new, completely original *and* just like everything else.

The paradox Dobson discovered applies to any company that tries to innovate, from toothpaste to smartphones. Integrating such paradox thinking into to new product development creates the kind of competitive advantage that companies profiled throughout this book enjoy.

In addition to innovation, leadership embodies myriad conflicting needs, such as confidence *and* humility, control *and* empowerment, grounded *and* visionary. Reinsurance Group of America (RGA) experienced major structural changes in 2008 and then again 2011. Because of these changes, new leadership paradoxes took shape for CEO Greig Woodring. Once owned by Metropolitan Life Insurance, RGA split off from MetLife in 2008 after expanding its global presence by adding new foreign offices. Then in 2011, it became a matrix organization and started to move toward more integrated systems instead of running like a loosely affiliated group of reinsurance companies. Control *and* empowerment emerged as central conflicting needs in his changing world. By exercising too much control, he could quash the entrepreneurial spirit of the individual company leaders. By empowering them too much, he would undermine the moves toward more coordinated behavior and goals.

Case Studies Prove the Power of Paradox Thinking

In this book, case studies of organizations help clarify the phases of a planning and implementation process that uses paradox thinking. Think of the process in terms of these macro steps:

1. Explore the types of paradoxes that your organization faces.
2. Evaluate when paradox thinking is necessary and when it's important to see choices as either one or another.
3. Envision the Aim, the Miss, and the possible positive and negative outcomes for your organization when you focus on each need separately and then together.
4. Energize the solution. Move out of the analysis stages and into actionable implementation to manage and leverage your paradoxes.
5. Equalize the execution. That is, put qualitative and quantitative measures in place to help indicate risk as you gauge progress.

Now visualize how these steps are connected and flow from one to the other, with the process repeating again and again. The steps have an energetic relationship. When practiced over time, this thinking becomes fluid and brings value instantly to your work life and your whole life.

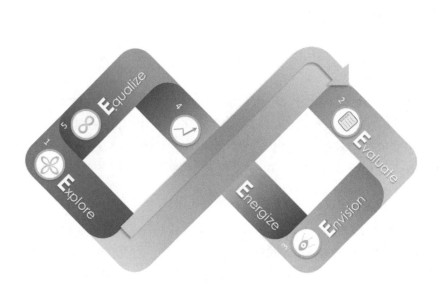

The case studies vary in size from a local not-for-profit to a global, multi-billion-dollar company. Exposure to their struggles and ultimate successes gives specific insights into how to put the process captured in the image to work in your own organization. You will see how real companies identified critical interdependent opposites and applied paradox thinking to them. As the stories develop in later chapters, you will also see how well they leveraged relationships between the two and implemented paradox thinking on an ongoing basis.

The four case studies introduced in this chapter and referred to in other parts of the book are a financial services company, an upscale hotel chain with annual sales of $2 billion, a not-for-profit healthcare organization with annual revenue of $20 billion, and a technology-related services company with annual sales of $5 million.

St. Louis–Based Financial Services Firm

A St. Louis–based financial services firm, which we will call St. Louis Finance, consists of more than 15,000 financial advisors who came together over the course of years through mergers with regional and national firms. The group provides asset management, estate planning, and related services.

A lot of change in the company occurred with upheaval in the financial services industry, and that had a tremendous impact on external opportunities and threats, and internal strengths and weaknesses. On the internal side, "Who's doing what?" bounced off the walls in many offices, with people wondering who had responsibility for creating the marketing strategy and who had responsibility for execution.

I provided guidance to the marketing executive team of St. Louis Finance throughout their 2013 and 2014 strategic planning effort. One of the fundamental elements at play in an organizational paradox is its ongoing nature, so in addition to an outside-in look at directionally where they needed to take their strategy, we discussed chronic issues and challenges for the group. This is the point at which we entered the "explore" stage of the process and determined that paradox thinking is necessary.

"What causes confusion and chaos for you?" I asked them.

I wanted them to look at their struggles and then accept that strategic planning would help them understand their struggles, not just rise above them. They needed to see what causes the struggles and then what sustains them—that is, what keeps them ongoing. Zeroing in on paradoxes is the way to do that.

There is no crisply defined formula for strategic planning, but there is one element every strategic planning exercise needs as it gets underway, and that is a common language. The one fundamental word when integrating paradox thinking into strategic planning is "and." Some elements of strategy are so interconnected, so dependent on one another and yet opposite, that they are like breathing. Examples are logic and creativity, deliberation and emergent action, revolution and evolutionary change, a focus on markets and consideration of internal resources.

Identifying key stakeholders and key partners set the context for articulating the main reason for coming together to tackle strategic issues—in a business environment, it's what I call the Aim. The Aim and its negative counterpart, the Miss, are discussed more in-depth beginning in Part II of the book. These are the absolute markers of whether an organization is managing to success or failure.

The Aim we identified for St. Louis Finance was "client growth." The Miss was "slow decline of business."

Fast-forward to several meetings later, where the executives identified six strategic priorities:

1. Growth through acquisition of successful financial advisors and their clients.
2. Direct, corporate cultivation of clients (customers).
3. Mining client/prospect data in order to know customers better.
4. Recruiting/developing talent in the company.
5. Exhibiting client/prospect data in order to share knowledge and demonstrate success.
6. Improvement and standardization of core services—that is, a focus on efficient processes.

At this point, we entered the "evaluate" part of the process; three sets of tensions took shape immediately. Through questions that guided conversation, my goal was to help them to look at those tensions and see them holistically. It was important for them to think of the list in terms of:

Growth through financial advisors *and* growth through direct contact with customers.

Emphasis on people (talent) *and* emphasis on process.

Gathering data to understand customers *and* sharing data to demonstrate success.

The group involved in the strategy process grew and no longer consisted of only the marketing executive team. Nine new people joined the group. Their job was to help build out the strategy and to be ambassadors of the strategy within the organization, as well as to act as key players in the implementation of the strategic plan.

In order to raise awareness of the fundamental "and" and to get buy-in from those who were new to the team, I expressed the three, opposing—yet linked—strategic pairs on a flip chart using the infinity loop, a symbol first used by Barry Johnson in his model to represent ongoing energy within the pair: ∞. So, for example, "talent" occupied the left side of the loop and "process" occupied the right, with the loop suggesting they are energetically connected. At the same time, I made it clear that the word "tension" had crept into all their conversations about these pairs.

And then I invited them to do a simple exercise:

"Inhale."

"Exhale."

"Inhale."

"Exhale."

"Inhale, and hold it."

Obviously, at some point, they wanted to exhale, but I didn't give them that instruction. Yet they exhaled because they couldn't continue to hold their breath. They got the point: You can't do one or the other if your Aim is to live. You have the same dynamic requirement with your company when it comes to these interdependent sets of opposites.

Particularly in strategic planning sessions, but also in meetings, participants tend to use "trap words" that hold them back from both/and thinking. Two of them are "priorities" and "agenda."

Priorities and agenda can get you stuck in either/or thinking because, by the nature of the words, they conjure up a this-then-that order, a first-then-second perception. That establishment of a hierarchy assigns more value to one possibility, which means another possibility has less value. I'm not saying that's invalid in all circumstances, but when you are considering paradoxes, it's essential to keep in mind that they are neither positive nor negative. They are equals—interdependent pairs. Priority thinking can take you to a choice, and that choice can imply either/or thinking and undermine your entire meeting or your entire strategic planning process.

The first success in the process of working with the St. Louis Finance group involved a change in their list of goals from six to five, with the two growth goals officially linked with an "and." Of course, the process must continue with action steps to move toward the Aim and a system of measuring how well you are managing the process. There are the "envision," "energize," and "equalize" steps that are covered in depth in Part II.

Livli Hotels

The context for this case study (in which the company name has changed and selected details have been disguised to protect confidentiality) is the recession that began in 2008. A company of any size faces radical changes if it loses 40 percent of its revenue stream overnight. That's essentially what happened to the Livli Hotels, a world-class hotel chain founded by a Scandinavian-American and headquartered in the U.S. Midwest. It had generated about $1.5 billion in annual sales prior to that year. Livli Hotels specializes in high-end services for business and leisure travelers; all locations offer some level of spa services as well as two or more restaurants.

Many consumers taking vacations scaled down their requirements for services. Business travelers had mandated reductions in travel spending; many companies simply replaced travel with computer-based alternatives such as Skype. Even companies that had regularly booked meetings at Livli Hotels around the world sought less-expensive alternatives.

Livli Hotels had thrived under the leadership of Karl A., son of the company founder, who became the CEO in 1998. He brought the family ethos of good customer service with him into the top job and maintained a company culture that was very much oriented to the guest relationship. Suddenly, that wasn't enough to weather the storm. Such a catastrophic loss of income required someone who knew how to do major surgery without killing the patient. Karl willingly stepped down, and the board of directors chose Ádo T. to take over on January 16, 2009.

Ádo had to cut people and spending, but not so deeply that there would be no one left to stay close to the client companies—even those companies that were no longer booking meetings—or that facilities maintenance and guest services would suffer. He did the job well, in part by staying on top of everything; he became a consummate micro-manager. With turnarounds such as this, it's important to get the new CEO in fast, yet he or she must be ready to take action as he or she starts reshaping the culture. Ádo's tenure lasted nearly four years, which was long enough to make an impact on the Livli culture. The most pronounced effect was that people became used to waiting until someone told them what to do. They expected micromanagement.

Ádo's tactics had the desired effect of returning the company to profitability. The leaner company kept up its pace of services with far fewer people, so productivity soared. But the time came when cut, cut, cut had to turn into grow, grow, grow. In December 2012, Dale G. took over as CEO.

Dale blasted in with four priority areas—all falling under the Aim of "dramatic growth":

1. Grow profitably.
2. Innovate in the area of guest services.
3. Build organizational capability.
4. Stay ahead in developing, key markets.

The Miss was summed up as "loss of market share."

Dale, a veteran of facilities management for several very large companies, was well-schooled in measures and metrics. He was used to measuring everything with an eye on quality, safety, high efficiency, and operational excellence. He brought this mentality with him and fueled it with a sense of urgency.

More than 6,000 people employed by Livli corporate heard what needed to happen. And then they waited for someone to tell them how to make it happen. They had spent four years in a reactive mode, a cautious and belt-tightening mode, a wait-until-the-CEO-tells-us-what-to-do mode. Actions ratcheted forward, slowly and steadily. In addition, many employees had developed a sense of complacency about customer relationships; they felt the quality of accommodations and amenities "spoke for themselves" so there was no need make changes based on guest feedback.

The new CEO assumed that when he said something people around him understood and would act on that understanding. He had a requirement for agility in all of the priority areas, but his pace of working and talking far exceeded what employees had become accustomed to.

Soon I received a call from the executive vice president for human resources, Liz P., who invited me to help focus efforts and hasten the pace of progress with an emphasis on building organizational capabilities. We needed to look underneath their issues at both what caused the problems and what were the source of the solutions.

Though there are several ways to bring to the surface a paradoxical relationship within an organization, one simply surfaced in my initial conversation with Liz. She expressed frustration with how long it takes to get anything done. The example she used was a new compensation approach. The process to revise it had been initiated three years earlier, and still no change had been put in place because the company was decentralized, and decisions made at the local level often trumped what people at the corporate level wanted to do. As she explained the interaction with the various individual hotels, the paradoxical relationship of global and local took shape for me. She needed to help people at the local level contribute to the big picture—that is, the hotel chain as a global player—*and* support their efforts to maintain autonomy and the character of local properties that their guests and client companies expected.

So where they were individually was critical for them locally, but the equally important corporate need was to move fast globally; they wanted top-of-mind awareness in all major markets. Livli Hotels could not build organizational capability without succeeding as a global *and* local company. And without that capability in place, it would not be possible to grow profitably, maintain a strong menu of imaginative services, and stay ahead in emerging, important markets.

Bringing the paradoxical relationship of global and local to the surface had an immediate impact on Liz's thinking. Perhaps the problem she had was not a structural one after all. We turned our attention to pulling her team into the conversation to see what would occur when we illuminated the "global" and "local" as interdependent concepts, with neither being positive or negative, neither being more important than the other. Inherent tensions between the two would then be seen as a natural part of a relationship of equals, rather than something to bury, beat down, or sidestep through *either* global *or* local dominance.

The team immediately had a fresh focus and renewed sense of engagement. They now saw a situation in which their company had a strong presence around the world *both* because of the standards established at the corporate level *and* because general managers at the individual properties had the freedom and creativity to manage that presence as they saw fit on the local level. Of course, that recognition didn't itself solve the problems that existed, but it did provide the foundation for a new way of working through them—the process I describe in later chapters.

Another immediate impact of pinpointing an organizational paradox like this is an increase in speed—the speed with which people make decisions and the speed with which they take actions toward a goal.

Affirm Health

Affirm Health (a real company with its name changed) has climbed to the summit of its industry during its 100-plus year history. It is one of the largest hospital systems in the United States, and in staying true to its mission to provide care regardless of ability to pay, it is a top provider of care to people who are uninsured or underinsured. The healthcare system that emerged as a result of the founders' efforts went through various names and structures through the years and became Affirm Health in the late 1990s.

In 2011, Affirm was a more-than-$11-billion operation, successful in terms of standards of care and intelligent growth, but suffering from sharp declines in revenue. Increases in charity care, escalating operating expenses, a slight shift away from reliance on commercial payers to government sources, and a drop in Medicaid rates combined to draw down the company's income from operations by 25 percent for 2011.

Affirm Health has a corporate structure that inherently involves two sets of needs because it is both an integrated healthcare system and a collection of hospitals. An executive could look at all of the interrelated needs and easily be overwhelmed. The path away from feeling overwhelmed is pairing them into conflicting needs. Once you begin to see a pattern of the interdependencies between the needs, addressing them becomes more straightforward.

My entrée into the myriad complex issues faced by Affirm involved relatively narrow focus on their capital spend. Some years ago, in a conversation I had with Affirm executives for the West Coast division, it became clear that something was missing—actually some*one* was missing. Distributed leadership had been the organization's model, with each individual CEO of a hospital traditionally having autonomy over how he or she spent and designed facilities in that market. Affirm leadership respected the decentralized model but realized they had no control over facilities development and maintenance. At the same time, they knew it was important to gain some control over the consistency of their brand

and the quality of their facilities for purposes of patient safety, family comfort, sustainability, and cost management, among other considerations.

The someone whom Affirm lacked was an executive with both big-picture perspective and facilities-management experience—a person to bridge the chasm between headquarters and the individual hospitals. They needed to create a role that would bring together centralized, corporate priorities and the distributed leadership needs of each facility in the system. If successful, that kind of person would play a pivotal role in helping preserve the autonomy of the hospital CEOs while ensuring that corporate standards for facilities influenced design and maintenance throughout the system. In 2008, Affirm created a senior position to lead a Facilities Task Force with the hope of accomplishing this coordination.

In examining the broader complex landscape of issues facing the entities that comprise Affirm Health, I surfaced a draft list of competing needs.

- Clinical needs—Identifying what is specifically necessary to provide quality patient care.
- Facilities needs—Maintaining structure without ad hoc patches or cheap fixes.
- Reducing costs—Cuts to improve bottom line in consideration of lower payments from government sources and an increase in charity cases.
- Increasing growth—Business, people (talent and numbers), and financial growth.
- Slow, steady growth—Pacing increases in consideration of resource constraints.
- Agility—Moving quickly to keep up with changes in the environment and changing needs of constituents.
- Focus on today—Addressing immediate needs of patients and caregivers.

- Preparation for tomorrow—The long-range plan means guaranteed access to care in all Affirm markets.

- Strategic plans—Vision and standards that are clearly articulated.

- Business plans—Hospitals have a clear sense of day-to-day actions.

- Mission—Staying true to a healing mission driven by compassion and dedication to care for those most in need.

- Margin—Watching the bottom line.

- Market brand—Establishing identity and boosting competitive edge.

- Company standard—Consistency and excellence.

- Headquarters perspective—A universal sense that the system is "our" project.

- Hospital perspective—A universal appreciation for the contribution of the individual facilities; "their" project mentality.

- Distributed leadership—Freedom of the hospital CEOs to serve their populations in the way they believe is best.

- Centralized control—Ensuring the use of best practices, adhering to budgets, and other corporate mandates.

- Asserting expertise—Individual and team confidence in skill areas.

- Nurturing relationship with managers/leaders—Regard for authority.

- Master plan—Sticking to the actions coming out of strategic vision.

- Responsiveness to needs—Rapid change, when necessary.

- Tight systems—Efficiency and adherence to protocols at the service end.

- Flexibility in care—Modifying rules and "staying loose" to customize care.

Chapter 4 shows how these separate needs came together as interdependent pairs of opposites. Most people who see 24 needs such as these take shape into interdependent pairs experience a palpable sense of optimism and relief. What seems unwieldy at first suddenly takes on a manageable form.

Mid-Sized Business (A Composite Case Study)

Following layoffs at a global, high-tech company, three people who had worked together in the federal division formed a business. They recognized a need in the market for temporary information technology employees for special projects and to support seasonal fluctuations in certain types of work. Though equal in their ownership of the business, the three partners decided that the computer engineer would serve as president. The other two partners had sales and marketing expertise. They called the company ITHRes.

Within six years, the company was generating $5 million in annual sales and had a full-time staff of 21; as many as 100 temporary employees worked for them at any given time. They worked a fairly tight region along the eastern seaboard, with a presence in four states.

The financial crisis of 2008 created cash-flow problems for them overnight, with their private sector clients effecting extended payment schedules and their government clients curtailing much of their contracting business. They then faced a chronic struggle very much like many other small and mid-sized businesses without access to new capital. They had a vision of growth at the same time that they were hampered by serious cash-flow issues.

Six of the 21 full-time staff members were IT professionals responsible for vetting temporary employees, interfacing with the clients' technical employees, and maintaining familiarity with client systems. Six others on staff focused on sales and marketing.

The technical team had what they thought was a great idea to grow the company. Their familiarity with client systems suggested to them that they should educate their clients about system improvements and acquisition of new IT products. The finance people determined that the margins on such an activity would exceed those of the temporary staffing activities.

The sales and marketing people thought this idea was off the mark and that launching an activity like that would confuse clients and prospects about what the company's core business was. They also feared that the vetting process for the temporary staff could be undermined. Their idea for growing the company was to secure contracts for large, short-term personnel needs, such as equipment installations for companies moving to new facilities. They had targeted several companies that specialized in moving businesses as possible partners.

The technical team felt sales and marketing were focusing too narrowly on the niche where the company had already had some success. They saw exciting new opportunities that could expand the company's scope into another market sector.

All the while, they faced the pressing cash-flow issue and had not adjusted to the delays in payments and, in some cases, non-payment.

That tension and back-and-forth conversation had dominated the company for the past four years of its 11-year life and was getting nowhere fast. To complicate the issue, the finance people were urging cost-cutting measures.

I asked questions about the growth process and whether it had been steady or had happened in fits and starts. It was the latter. The company was lucky early in landing two very big contracts, after which it added staff and expanded geographically. Realizing their up-and-down history was a dysfunctional way to grow a company, they now sought ways to achieve "steady growth," which is what I captured as the Aim in my work with them.

My questions about the values of the two teams, as well as their greatest fears, moved us toward identifying a paradoxical need that could galvanize them.

The technical team's greatest fear was that their expertise would continue to be underplayed to the detriment of the company's growth plans. The sales and marketing team feared their messages and branding efforts would lose their effectiveness if the company diversified. On the values side, they both appreciated the standards of technical excellence that the company was known for, but each had a slightly different view of how they showed up. The technical team felt it rested with them and their expertise; the sales and marketing team focused on the skills and experience of the cadre of temps the company placed.

I focused on the tensions *within* their greatest fears and values. Both fears and values were present in the relationship between stability and change. There were some exciting opportunities associated with change, but the risks were huge, considering the uncertainty about cash flow. There was a level of predictability in staying the course, and it likely could keep the organization on an even keel financially, but that didn't seem to offer a chance to grow the company in terms of brand or revenue.

The question that got the two teams eager to work with each other and forge ahead was, How it is possible to maintain stability *and* effect change?

The chapters that follow will reveal how the stories of these companies developed and will present other client case studies in industries that include high tech, healthcare, manufacturing, not-for-profit arts, and financial services. These companies all had to adopt paradox thinking as a competitive necessity.

As a framework for strategic and tactical thinking, a paradox approach to business represents an exhilarating set of possibilities. It is a radical way to solve problems and exploit opportunities.

Chapter 2

The ABCs of Using
Paradox Thinking

"How wonderful that we have met with
a paradox. Now we have some hope of
making progress."

—Niels Bohr,
Nobel Prize–winning physicist

As you explore paradoxes and start to identify those that are active in your organization, consider this: Paradoxes are tied to a greater purpose—what I call the Aim. The Aim illuminates the necessity of the pair(s) of interdependent opposites; managing both well is vital if you want to achieve your Aim.

It's easy to say that stability and change are opposites, but those concepts become linked and gain meaning as a pair when they refer to the growth of any business. Take a consumer business, for example. The company must maintain stability in order to sustain customer trust, and it must change in order to meet evolving needs in the marketplace. Total commitment to stability means that competitors overtake it. Constant change undermines branding and reputation because the corporate identity is so fluid.

Types of Paradoxes

Paradoxes are all around us. They are like gravity—inevitable. Three examples are:

- Inhale *and* exhale—In order to live, you have to do both.

- Part *and* whole—A person is an individual; at the same time, the individual is part of something greater, such as a family, team, community, nation, and species.

- Activity *and* rest—If a person tries to be only active or to stay at rest, the outcome is death, so we have no choice but to do both.

An organizational equivalent of inhale and exhale is that a company needs to satisfy the customer and satisfy the shareholder. The part and whole consideration is that a company is never alone in an industry. And the organizational equivalent of activity and rest is stability and change.

In contrast to the inevitable paradoxes, there are those that are situational. For example:

- Situation—Parenting: Teach my child *and* let her learn herself.

- Situation—Firefighter: Follow formal processes *and* be flexible to the emerging needs.

- Situation—Functional leader: Focus on my function *and* focus on the organization.

Often unaware, we opt into these chosen paradoxes by becoming involved in certain situations. We can avoid them only if we avoid the context in which they occur.

In choosing to start a business that involves employees, a founder becomes involved in paradoxes of leadership and organization. Recognition of paradox is crucial. For example, the interdependent pair of global and local faced by Livli Hotels wouldn't exist if the structural model for the company were a single-nation company. Instead, the company decided on a business model that made "global and local" a key pair for them.

Paradoxes don't only come in pairs. As the complexity of the situation increases, so does the complexity of paradoxes. Sometimes issues are nested within each other or stacked on top of one another:

▶ Simple pairs: An example is "learning from self" and "learning from others" in the context of pursuing career-development goals.

▶ Complex sets: An example is "manufacturing and legal and marketing"; in a matrix organization, it might be "product and geography and function."

▶ Nested paradoxes: A pair of interdependent opposites contains another pair of interdependent opposites nested within it. There is no set limit to how many pairs might be nested within another. It could be one, or many.

A simple example is the pair "work and home." Nested inside of work is "my needs and my company's needs"; nested inside of home is "my needs and my family's needs." Drilling down even further, we might discover another paradox on the work side, such as "contribution through initiative and contribution through followership."

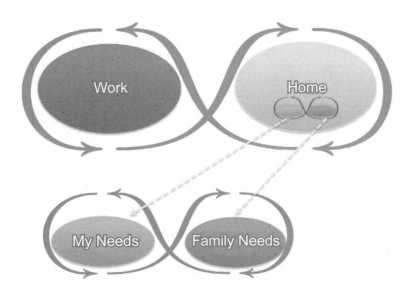

Another example would be a leader paying attention to the conditional respect and unconditional respect paradox. In giving conditional respect, the leader recognizes good work and holds people accountable for poor work; otherwise she isn't getting the fullness of "conditional respect." Another pair that could be nested in the conditional side is "feedback in the moment and feedback over time," meaning providing input and/or criticism on a real-time basis about a project and giving feedback based on long-term observation of job performance.

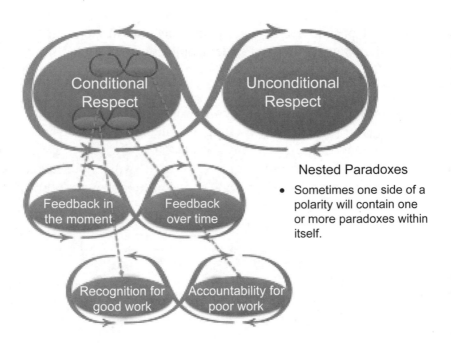

Conditional Respect

Unconditional Respect

Feedback in the moment

Feedback over time

Recognition for good work

Accountability for poor work

Nested Paradoxes

- Sometimes one side of a polarity will contain one or more paradoxes within itself.

An example from the world of public relations is the goal of a PR professional to serve the publicity needs of clients _and_ have news sources perceive him as a reliable source of information. A nested paradox on the "serve the client" side is the conflicting set of needs to get publicity for the client and to prevent publicity from occurring if it might make the client look bad.

▶ Stacked paradoxes: Stacking refers to paradoxes that have a vertical relationship with other paradoxes. How you manage one affects the one below it.

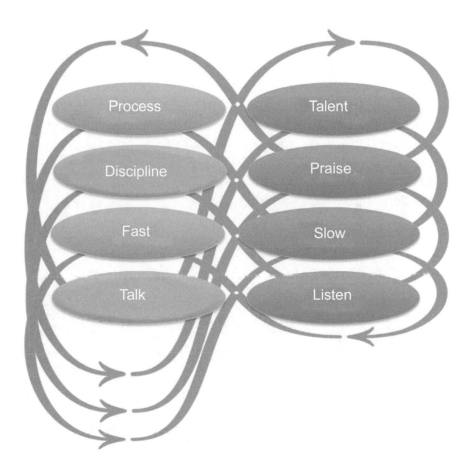

If nesting was about "magnification," then stacking is about "amplification": How does the downward energy of putting too much attention on one part of the pair amplify the downward energy from putting too much attention on only one part of another pair? Think of a trampoline with two people holding hands and bouncing on it, hitting and peaking at the same time. They break their grasp and starting hitting at different times, ultimately having a completely opposite rhythm. The dip down on the trampoline increases dramatically, as does the height each jumper achieves. In resonance terms, the same driving forces produce large amplitude oscillations.

Case in point: Jack had just retired from the Air Force with the rank of general when he got a job heading the sales division of a company that did a lot of work with the United States Defense Department. He brought a strong sense of process to the job; at the same time, he knew the value of empowering and encouraging the talented people around him. He hired a human resources director who related far more to the general's appreciation for process, however. Ultimately, the division's over-focus on process gave discipline more weight than praise and punishment more weight than incentives. The emphasis had a demoralizing effect and triggered the departure of many employees.

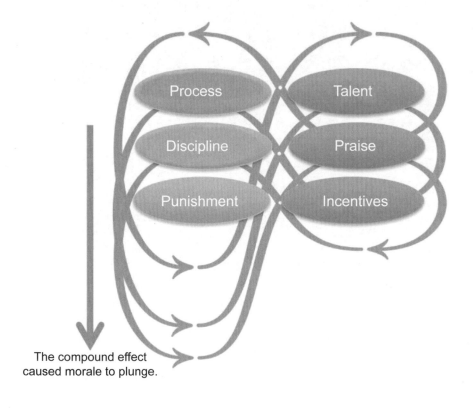

The compound effect
caused morale to plunge.

Categories of Paradox

In business, categories of paradoxes often fall into three camps: leadership, organizational, and human behavior. This list, however, doesn't come close to capturing all of the possible categories, or suggesting the many potential sub-categories of paradoxes.

Examples of leadership paradoxes are:

+ Task focus *and* relationship focus.
+ Candor *and* diplomacy.
+ Individual *and* team.

Examples of organizational paradoxes are:

+ Centralized coordination *and* decentralized initiatives.
+ Stability *and* change.
+ External orientation *and* internal orientation.

Examples of human behavior paradoxes are:

+ Qualitative thinking *and* quantitative thinking.
+ Strategic behavior *and* tactical behavior.
+ Self focus *and* other focus.

Most of the following paradoxes are real conflicting needs of companies and non-profit organizations that I've worked with. The list is meant to provoke initial thinking about the nature of tensions in your organization and how they may be paired up, depending on your organizational Aim.

Business Strategy

As you consider sweeping questions such as "What business are you really in?" and "What do you want your company to be when it grows up?" you will likely recognize some, or even all, of these paradoxes:

+ Logic *and* creativity.
+ Short term *and* long term.
+ Known *and* unknown.

- Competition _and_ cooperation.
- Safety _and_ risk.
- Environmental _and_ organizational assessment.
- Formulation _and_ implementation.
- Mission focus _and_ margin focus.

Using the composite case study introduced in Chapter 1, let's look at how these paradoxes have practical meaning for a company. The technology professionals at ITHRes wanted to explore new territory—to get creative—while the sales and marketing people felt the most logical strategy was to expand on current operations. Related to that conflict was the teams' disagreement on whether to go for the bigger margins associated with the creative approach or the mission-focus of the sales and marketing team's approach. It's possible to go down this list and, similarly, match concepts to real business strategy challenges at ITHRes—and anywhere else.

It's important to note that these are simply concepts rather than the unique words you need to assign your business strategy paradoxes. They are the generic way of describing whatever your organization is facing.

Business Design

These concepts relate to what your organization looks like:

- Vertical _and_ horizontal.
- Individual _and_ organizational.
- Hard structures (business model structure) _and_ soft structures (performance management process).

Put these paradoxes in the context of Livli Hotels, for example. You might immediately think of the tensions related to a company that is designed to connect closely with customers in different regions and at the same time needs to have consistency in certain standards and procedures system-wide. Individual general managers must have sufficient autonomy while they adhere to corporate best practices.

Core Business Process

The success of your organization depends not only on departmental/ team performance, but also on departmental/team interrelationships. The paradoxes related to those factors are tied to your core business process:

- ◗ Marketing *and* sales.
- ◗ Succession management *and* performance management.
- ◗ Input *and* output.
- ◗ Integrated *and* discrete.
- ◗ Stability *and* change.
- ◗ Standardized *and* customized.

In the case study of St. Louis Finance, I introduced the marketing and sales issue. The group needs to cultivate clients by increasing awareness among potential customers as well as directly selling the portfolio management services, which financial advisors (FAs) provide. The former is really a marketing function that needs to happen in balance and concurrently with the sales function associated with the FAs. As a corollary, reaching out to potential customers involves a standardized message; St. Louis Finance is promoting a brand. On the other hand, the interaction that FAs have with clients is customized. As a third example of a core business paradox faced by St. Louis Finance, their "stability *and* change" challenge is captured in the need to build financial trust through consistency and reliability and, at the same time, offer their clients the prospect of exciting financial growth through a diversity of offerings.

Corporate Culture/Shared Values

Organizations are collections of human beings with (theoretically) a common purpose. Many factors are integral to how we go about achieving that common purpose, and many of them reflect normal tensions, such as:

- Formal *and* informal.
- Plan-oriented *and* action-oriented.
- Traditional *and* innovative.
- Company *and* community.
- Team *and* individual.
- Customer focus *and* employee focus.
- Mission *and* margin.
- Quantity *and* quality.

Affirm Health's mission is to serve the healthcare needs of all people, including those who need assistance with paying. At the same time, the organization's vision statement refers to a strong, vibrant healthcare business, which is something that cannot be accomplished without decent margins. The analogous tension between addressing needs of the community and corporate, or hospital, needs is also central for Affirm.

Although the concept of organizational culture first appeared in 431 BC, when it was thought the Spartan war could win through strong unified teamwork, the concept didn't make an appearance in business until the mid-'80s. The business world was intrigued with the idea that a business might have a culture, but didn't know what to do with this. There have been 100+ definitions of culture, yet of very little value to the average manager. Questions asked included:

Where does it come from?

How do you change it—and why?

How do you measure it?

Daniel R. Denison (author of *Corporate Culture and Organizational Effectiveness*), who is well known for his work in organizational culture, has looked deeply at how culture affects market share, sales growth, quality, return on investment, employee satisfactory, innovation, and other key factors related to corporate success. More than 900 businesses of all sizes and sectors participated in the development of his model—rooted in workplace behaviors.

At the heart of any corporate culture are beliefs and assumptions. A new organizational leader who does not acknowledge that, and tries to bring about a culture merely through behavior modification, will fail. The culture will either remain what it had been and be carried forward by others perceived as leaders throughout the organization, or it will morph a bit but not transform. The new leader could spend years wondering why his vision for growth and employee engagement, for example, is not being realized fully. The fact that he did not come to terms with the factors that drive human behavior—beliefs and assumptions—are a good reason why he failed.

The following chart is an abbreviated version of one created by Denison to help organizations understand how their culture affects their behavior and outcomes:

Denison's model does what many other culture models fail to do. It embraces, rather than ignores, the basic paradoxes managers and leaders face in their business. You need to pay attention to seemingly conflicting objectives. A company with an external focus and emphasis on stability has a culture with a truly shared mission. In working with one of my energy company clients, my colleagues and I discovered that the company scored very high in this quadrant. They also scored high in the quadrant defined by the relationship between stability and internal focus, which means that their culture held consistency as an important value. Another organization that likely would score similarly if analyzed using the Denison model is Affirm Health.

An organization with an external focus on emphasis on flexibility, or change, would have a culture of adaptability. One with an internal focus and flexibility would reflect a culture that engenders employee empowerment and has a team orientation.

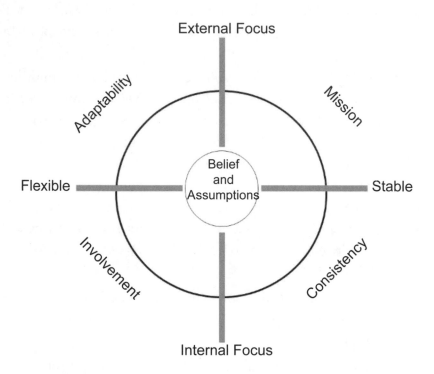

Consider all of these factors through the lens of paradox. If an organization goes through a cultural self-assessment such as Denison's and realizes that scores are not balanced in the quadrants, they may have (a) an important revelation regarding company performance in key areas and (b) a life-saving warning that focus on external over internal, stability over change (or vice versa) is causing certain performance problems.

Global Culture

Authors Fons Trompenaars and Charles Hampden-Turner have written extensively about understanding diversity in global business. In their book, _Riding the Waves of Culture_, they offer "seven intercultural dimensions" of working with people of other cultures. These dimensions are paradoxes that capture the major differences between cultures. A given culture may be closer to one part of the pair of opposites rather than the other, so harnessing the energetic relationship inherent in these tensions is vital in team-building for a global enterprise.[1]

▶ Rule-making *and* exception-finding.

▶ Self-interest/Personal fulfillment *and* group interest/Social concern. (The authors refer to this as "individualism and communitarianism."[2])

▶ Emotions inhibited *and* emotions expressed.

▶ Preferences for precise, singular "hard" standards *and* preference for pervasive, patterned "soft" processes. The authors' simple way of expressing this pair is "specificity and diffusion," but I'd like you to think of the long version in terms of four stacked paradoxes. This will not only help to clarify the concept of stacking, but also cause you to think about how you may be stacking concepts without even realizing it. The stacked pairs are precise *and* pervasive, singular *and* patterned, hard *and* soft, standards *and* processes.

▶ Control and effective direction comes from within *and* control and effective direction comes from outside (an alternate for this would be inner directed *and* outer directed).

▶ Status earned through success and track record *and* status ascribed to a person's potential (or this pair could be called achievement *and* ascription; the latter refers to advantages we didn't earn, such as family and innate intelligence).

▶ Time is conceived of as a race with passing increments *and* time is conceived of as a dance with circular iterations (the alternative: sequential *and* synchronous).

Leading People

With a constantly shifting landscape, leading and managing the valued contributions of talent in the organization are more critical to company success than ever before. Though needs vary among companies and circumstances, leaders at all levels have to be able to define the goals and objectives of the business, and provide enablement and motivation for the organization to succeed.

People at any level of an organization can lead others, yet a number of these paradoxes suggest that they apply more to someone in a formal leadership role rather than an informal one:

- Leading *and* following.
- Directive *and* empowering.
- Speaking *and* listening.
- Task *and* relationship.
- Boss *and* friend.
- Unconditional *and* conditional respect.
- Care for self *and* care for others.
- Loose decision-making *and* tight decision-making.
- Strategic *and* tactical.

Referring back to the story of RGA and CEO Greig Woodring, briefly noted in Chapter 1, the issue of leading an organization undergoing massive structural changes amplifies the paradoxes faced by a leader. People around the CEO and other senior executives probably feel unsettled; they need to be spoken to and listened to, directed and empowered. Woodring's ability to maintain balance is not only a make-or-break challenge for him in his position, but it also has ramifications for the company as a whole.

The following leadership paradoxes are in a sub-category we might call "competency pairs." Competency pairs are often paradoxes that become critical in hiring situations or promotions. In evaluating a candidate for a job, you want to assess his strengths, of course, but if a person is over the top in one strength, that might signal an imbalance in competencies. He might excel in strategic management, for example, and be seriously deficient in tactical abilities. You want to consider the candidate's full set of capabilities with these interdependent opposites in mind or you could undermine organizational strength. In the example of the retired general cited in the explanation of stacked paradoxes, he failed to evaluate his new manager's ability to balance competencies.

As a result, the weight of process, discipline, and punishment led to a steady departure of personnel from the department.

- Change agent *and* team player.
- Innovative thinker *and* implementation driver.
- Strategic visionary *and* operations leader.
- Customer advisor *and* employee engagement builder.

Leading Teams

The value of teams and teamwork has been a dominant perspective in business with increasing attention since the mid-'80s. The necessity for teams stretches beyond organizational performance requirements. Today they have become the social, economic, and psychological glue of organizational life.

Effective leaders of teams appreciate the paradoxes that live in the dynamic of teamwork and ultimately team success. First, leaders need to be clear about the purpose of the team. For example, is the purpose execution or innovation? Tightly led works better with teams focused on execution, whereas greater autonomy is necessary for teams expected to deliver innovation and/or improvement. Effective leaders find balance as they manage such key paradoxes as these effectively:

- Hands-off leadership *and* hands-on leadership.
- Individual recognition of team members *and* collective appreciation for team results.
- Divergent thinking *and* convergent thinking.
- Structured meetings *and* flexible agendas.
- Fluid creativity *and* controlled implementation.
- Macro perspective *and* micro understanding.
- Fact-based decision-making *and* assumptive decision-making.

In *Rangers Lead the Way*, a former Army Ranger and founder of the experiential learning program Leading Concepts makes the point that

Rangers are expected to be leaders _and_ team players. Through simulated Ranger experiences in the wilderness, he has introduced people at all levels in companies to the value of that paradox in corporate life. In this story, he vividly illustrates how Rangers—functioning as leaders and team members—took action moment-by-moment during the invasion of Panama in 1989:

> During the invasion in Panama, we formed lots of subteams on the fly...about 700 Rangers penetrated Rio Hato within a couple of minutes.
>
> On the way to my objective, I had to go about a mile and a half to my rally point. Along the way, I ran into all kinds of Rangers. We identified each other through a unique pattern we made with our silhouettes. We made nets and put them over our hard helmets (K-pots). We called them Bob Marley hats (after the Reggae master) because it looked as though we had dreadlocks. At night, if you saw the "dreadlocks" bouncing, you knew just by the silhouette that the person was a friendly. If you wanted to verify that, you could use the "running password," bulldog. When you heard "bulldog" back, you knew the guy was in the same Mission brief as you were.
>
> Using these codes, I became part of four different fire teams in a distance of a mile and a half, and we all assumed whatever roles were needed to complement each other in a 360 as we moved along. If we were traveling one way and a Ranger's objective was a nearby bridge, we'd drop him off at his rally point and move on. At times, we were down to three men, but then we'd move a little farther to where another guy landed and pick him up, always shaping up so we have 360 security. We formed and disbanded teams along the entire route.[3]

The actions of these Rangers reflect structure and flexibility, creativity and controlled implementation, and macro perspective and micro understanding—with all interdependent pairs in balance.

Talent/Staff/People

These paradoxes apply to people at every level of the organization:

- People *and* process.
- Being *and* doing.
- Home life *and* work life.
- Accepting *and* challenging ideas.
- Candor *and* diplomacy in communication.
- Individual *and* team.

Restructuring/Merging/Acquisition

These paradoxes are intimately linked with many others concerning culture, leadership, business strategy, and integration. They are especially key during restructuring or merger/acquisition activities:

- Knowing the inside of your organization *and* knowing the outside of your organization.
- Providing direction *and* inviting participation.
- Combining the best of your past and present *and* envisioning compelling future possibilities.
- Organization achieving its full potential *and* people achieving their full potential.
- Planning for your future *and* being in your future now.
- Inquiring about what others believe *and* advocating for what you believe.

Nature/Nurture

Assessments measure those attributes that differentiate one type of talent from another, those that may distinguish someone as a high-value contributor in one setting or role more than another. The following instruments illuminate the innate paradoxes that we all have and link observable behavior to those paradoxes.

Fundamentally, what these tools do is start with sets of opposites, even though human beings are hardly ever extremely one way or another. From the organization's perspective, they complement other types of screening used in hiring and promoting. From the individual's perspective, they help us understand the interdependencies within us so we are better able to manage ourselves in different situations.

Thinking Preferences: Herrmann Brain Dominance Instrument (HBDI)

◆ Cognitive orientation _and_ emotional orientation.

◆ Left brain _and_ right brain.

Work Style Preferences: DISC

◆ Task _and_ people.

◆ Formal _and_ informal.

Personality Traits: Myers-Briggs Type Indicator (MBTI)

◆ Extraversion _and_ introversion.

◆ Sensing _and_ intuition.

◆ Thinking _and_ feeling.

◆ Judging _and_ perceiving.

Learning Styles: Kolb Learning Styles

◆ Concrete experience _and_ abstract conceptualization.

◆ Reflective observation _and_ active experimentation.

Management Research Group (MRG) Leadership Styles: Leadership Effectiveness Analysis (LEA) (sample pairs)

◆ Conservative _and_ innovative.

◆ Management focus _and_ production focus.

◆ Consensual _and_ persuasive.

In understanding more about the paradoxes within oneself—and the fact that we tend to have a preference for one part of the pair more than the other—we can get some keen insights into how paradoxes influence our behavior. For example, let's focus for a moment on HBDI, which I use quite often with clients when there is a need to better understand behaviors in a team.

HBDI was developed by Ned Herrmann to measure thinking preferences. It consists of 120 questions; the answers help determine which of the model's four styles of thinking is a dominant preference. Herrmann developed it because he was curious about his own duality of preference, something he began to understand as he was studying the brain at Cornell University. With a major in both physics and music, which suggests why he felt he had a duality of preference, he later became head of management education for General Electric.

The whole brain model he created captures the four major types of thinking preferences in four quadrants:

The Whole Brain Model

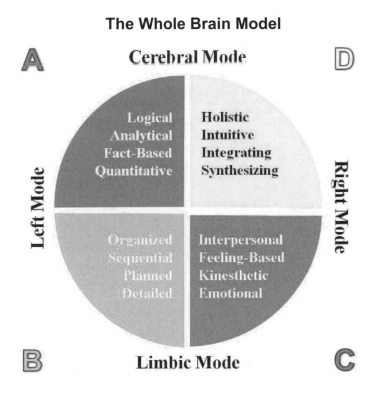

© 1986–1998, Ned Hermann Group

More than one style may be dominant at once in this model. A person may be dominant in both analytical and sequential styles of thinking, for example, but be weaker in interpersonal or imaginative modes. He is essentially stretching in different directions, depending on the circumstances, so the percentages describing how dominant someone is in a particular area could change.

Sample Profile
Jane Doe

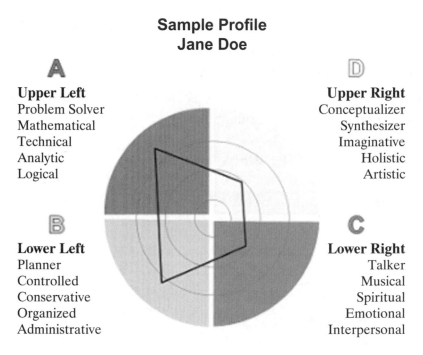

A

Upper Left
Problem Solver
Mathematical
Technical
Analytic
Logical

D

Upper Right
Conceptualizer
Synthesizer
Imaginative
Holistic
Artistic

B

Lower Left
Planner
Controlled
Conservative
Organized
Administrative

C

Lower Right
Talker
Musical
Spiritual
Emotional
Interpersonal

All people use all styles to varying degrees. The instrument provides visual easy-to-read pictures of an individual's, pair's, or organization's mental or thinking preferences. Questions focus on the past, present, and future. Extensive and ongoing validation studies have been performed and the research found that diversity of thinking styles exists in any organization.

HBDI yields useful data on thinking preferences, and can help surface conflicting needs and tensions simply by spotlighting where the focus of people lies and how they approach problems. For example, a team composed of people who are change averse, and perhaps led by someone who has the same predisposition, will consider maintaining status quo and stability a highly valued option. It may not even be possible for them to consider ways of transforming the organization or altering processes already in place. By looking at the assessment data, this kind of issue will pop out. The assessment data also removes any sense of negative judgment or guilt about why the team didn't explore change. They behaved in a way that's consistent with their DNA, that's all!

Global Business Trends

In this grouping, examples of paradoxes fall within a number of sub-categories, such as:

▶ Social everything:
  ◆ High tech *and* high touch.
  ◆ Spontaneous immediacy *and* intentional delay.
▶ Redefining consumer value:
  ◆ Needs for today *and* needs for tomorrow.
  ◆ B2C *and* C2C.
▶ Distributed everything:
  ◆ Distributed knowledge network *and* single-server hosting.
  ◆ Single idea *and* viral attraction.
▶ Frontiers of technology:
  ◆ New machines reshaping work *and* new machines eliminating work.
  ◆ Technology adoption driving information proliferation *and* technology creativity increasing long-lasting impact on culture.
▶ People resources:
  ◆ Abundance of talent *and* shortage of talent to meet needs.
  ◆ Demonstrated performance *and* future potential.
  ◆ Stellar career *and* portable career *and* portfolio career.

▶ From profit to purpose:

   ◗ Material success _and_ meaningful life.

   ◗ Work-life balance _and_ work-life enjoyment.

▶ The security challenge:

   ◗ Compliance _and_ choice.

   ◗ Privacy _and_ accessibility.

To help you cultivate a deeper understanding of how pairs reflect chronic organizational issues, I spotlight two of the paradoxes under "Restructuring/Merging/Acquisition."

Knowing the Inside of Your Organization _and_ Knowing the Outside of Your Organization: This paradox arises from concurrent concerns about core competencies and how the organization compares to competitors.

An organization needs to know what its valuable, unique internal strengths are at present, as well as which of those strengths will be meaningful to the organization going forward. Based on what competitors are doing and what is changing in the competitive environment, some of the things the organization does well today may not even be relevant tomorrow.

Planning for Your Future _and_ Being in Your Future Now: In meeting with the advisory board of Archbishop University, composed of business leaders and members of the university's senior administrative body, one of the business leaders said, "When we're developing strategy, we always have—front and center—what we're best at and what we're known for." Archbishop University is a university that wants to be known as the finest Catholic university in the nation, but its reputation had fallen short. It was not, as the board member pointed out, because the university lacked anything in terms of quality. It was because of marketing. So the vision for the future could not happen unless the university lived in the future by projecting itself as the finest Catholic university in the nation.

The board member summed it up well to his colleagues on the faculty: "If you think you're the finest Catholic university, then you have to tell people that you are!"

Another pair worth highlighting to clarify the process is "high tech *and* high touch" under the sub-category of "social everything." We have to be careful about how we use technology to communicate. That caution applies to business and personal situations. So we may rely on a mobile device to send a message about an action, but that message may be lacking in conveying the emotion related to the action. "Meet now A4" would send the directive to meet in conference room A4 immediately. What else? There is no why and there is no why not. The "high touch" is potentially lacking. Variables include how well you know the person (and vice versa), the context of the communication, and so much more, so there is no hard and fast rule about the degree to which you can achieve high touch through efficient, digital communication.

Going back to the discussion of types of paradoxes, particularly nesting and stacking, the "high touch" part of the paradox contains several nested paradoxes. They go from "listening and speaking," for example, to something a little more complex like "advocacy and inquiry." In the "high touch" part of the pair, there is also a common, conflicting need to use technical jargon and rely on ordinary language to promote understanding; this paradox applies to many industries. Technical language communicates specific needs and ideas, but it's also a barrier to understanding for many people.

This "high tech and high touch" pair of conflicting needs strikes at the heart of any educational institution that provides online learning programs. They face the mission to use the World Wide Web as an educational medium at the same time they aim to provide personal mentoring to students. Do they use their virtual presence in a way that goes beyond pushing information and into pulling in comments, questions, and connections?

Sometimes it's not necessary to connect the pairs so definitely and so specifically, but to ensure there is coverage of the pairs within an organization. Consider "change agent _and_ team player" in the prior list of competency pairs. They are tiered in terms of people: individual contributor, leader/manager, senior leader. In other words, everybody up and down the line needs to be a change agent and a team player. If each one isn't both, then achieving the set of expressed goals for the organization may not happen.

The further and deeper you understand why and how to view your needs as paradoxes, the easier it is use your new lens all the time. Think of the ability to perceive paradoxes like Google Glass: You have more information about what's in front of you and have a way of capturing what you're seeing so you can remember it better and share it.

Paradoxes Related to Business Life-Cycle

Some key paradoxes link directly to business life-cycle. Depending on whether your company is just getting started or it's been around for decades, it naturally faces some different tensions. Here is a summary of them.

Incubator

You are in the idea stage, asking yourself questions such as: What does our ownership look like? What does our structure look like? What kind of advisors do we need to pull in? You have no proof yet that anything will go forward, but you are taking actions with the intent that it will. Paradoxes you face include:

- Planning for broad success _and_ responding to niche opportunities.
- Focusing on my business plan _and_ being watchful to market needs.

Startup

Your company now legally exists, with some products and/or services already available to customers. You have some initial customers, and one of your challenges is ensuring that your products and services are meaningful to your customers and prospects. That issue gives rise to the second of the following two paradoxes

- Establishing marketing presence *and* conserving cash flow.
- Profitable needs that you have *and* profitable needs that your customers/prospects have.

Growth (emergent)

Revenues are rising, and you see increases in the number of customers and business opportunities. The significance of competition has now taken on a new dimension, with pressures to get an edge mounting. In short, you face a growing number of complications and demand related to your business every day. Paradoxes associated with this stage include a complex paradox related to your need to keep high-performing senior leaders in place, recruiting new people with the skills you require, and motivating your current team to stay energized:

- Focusing on growth plans *and* managing current costs.
- Having the talent to uncover client/customer needs *and* having the talent to respond to those needs.
- Retaining top talent *and* attracting new talent *and* engaging talent across the board.

Established

When your company is rising and thriving company, you have market share, and are recognized as viable business, a whole new set of paradoxes come into play. You have some related to the fact of having repeat customers and a recognized brand; continued sales growth, even if it's not explosive trend line; and pride in your sustainable development and solid business practices. At this stage, you also are likely to have a founder and/or senior leadership that have been in place during the rise, patting themselves on the back—creating the opposite need for them to pat others on the back.

- Self (founder/leaders focused on self) *and* others (founder/leaders focused on organization).
- Delivering on current customer needs *and* awareness of changing needs signaled in the market.
- Taking the time for making improvements and changes *and* increasing efficiency/productivity and speed in responding to customer needs.
- Mission *and* margin.

Regarding the last one, people need to know why they affiliated with the organization in the first place. They also need to be mindful of what they are contributing to its success in addition to hitting good margins to ensure continuation of the mission for years to come. An established organization can breed matter-of-factness about success and why it's worth working hard to sustain. People need to ask the question: "Am I getting complacent?" It can be very easy to be so consumed with departmental or project priorities that people lose sight of the organizational mission, but being disconnected from it can undermine success of the whole company.

Expansion

At this stage, you are extending the business into new markets, penetrating new distribution channels, finding new revenue—lots of "new" that could lure your attention to the future and make you lose sight of the "old"—that is, where you have been and where you currently are. You are hungry to gain more market share, but a preoccupation with the challenge for planning and starting up complementary and divergent aspects of the business could pull your operation out of balance unless you manage the paradoxes, including:

- Current products/services *and* complementary products/ services.

- Organic growth *and* acquisitive growth.

- Local footprint *and* national/global footprint.

- Entrepreneurial spirit *and* adherence to the need for systematic and regulated growth.

The last paradox could also be expressed as "freedom *and* control." Expansion invariably involves these two tensions over and over again. In a joint venture, for example, you have to focus on control issues as the deal is structured all the way though the tactical aspects of managing it. You need to care for the business where the joint venture is located, while not sub-optimizing the whole business by paying too much attention to the local business or new market activities. You might also have to deal with control issues related to laws and regulations in another jurisdiction. Mixed into that may be issues with cultural practices and regulating how staff interacts with customers, and/ or how products and services are presented to potential customers. All the while, you still want freedom in terms of how you bring the company forward throughout the expansion period—which lasts forever if you manage your paradoxes well!

Mature

You've arrived! Your business is successful with a solid customer base and good cash flow, yet competition is fierce. Eventually sales will drop off if you don't manage your paradoxical situations well. It's time to set the plans to attack, defend, and retreat. In itself, this is a complex paradox inside the discipline of controlling costs and still seeking growth potential for your organization. You have sound business practices, but the competition you face is growing fiercer; revenue declines are showing up and you see a sales decline with variable profits and weakening cash flow.

You face an either/or question: Renew the business or exit?

Choosing to renew the business means investigating opportunities while tightening the belt on costs. If you choose to try to breathe new life into the company, your complex paradox is searching for opportunities *and* taking care of current business *and* having discipline to manage costs/new demands.

Exit (Sunset)

You now need to take stock of what your company's best value is in the market, to do a valuation of the business and answer a critical either/or question: Do you sell all or a part of the business, or do you shut down the whole business, or perhaps a division of it? A key paradox is manage financial *and* psychological aspects of business.

Shared Paradoxes

As a final note on types of paradoxes, I want to share some examples of paradoxical conditions that all businesses face at some level or another. You will undoubtedly notice that many of the concepts are woven into the language of the paradoxes listed previously, if not actually stated this way:

- Self and other.
- Lead and follow.
- Process and people.
- Centralized and decentralized.
- Control and freedom.
- Fast and slow.
- Today and tomorrow.
- Change and stability.
- External focus and internal needs.
- Investing in growth and managing cost.
- Margin and mission.

In this list, I have intentionally arranged left and right to reflect organizational mistakes I have seen many times before. Go down the list and focus on the left part of the pair; you see terms that describe a high-risk, high-growth company with an aggressive leader who pushes for short-term profit—very task/output oriented. Focusing on the right, you may well think of some sales-/service-centered organizations you've dealt with—very relationship oriented. Any organization that consistently manages these pairs with that kind of extreme left-versus-right imbalance will not survive—no exceptions.

Chapter 3

Identifying Paradoxes in Any Organization

"A lot of people never use their
initiative because no one told them to."
—Banksy, British graffiti artist

When you're learning to play the piano, you need to learn the fundamentals before you can play a song. This is analogous to the process of identifying paradoxes in your organization: You go through the process so that paradox thinking can come alive and have practical value for you.

Exploring the Paradoxes an Organization Faces

Identifying paradoxes is a process of simplification. You start with a collection of competing needs, and use paradox thinking to understand the relationship between them and organize them for practical benefit. There are four basic ways to identify paradoxes, and anyone reading this book should be able to use them all. Drawing out the fears and values of the situation is one of four ways I use to bring interdependent opposite pairs to the surface. Another is zeroing in on chronic tensions or struggles. A third is identifying from-to relationships—where the organization has come from and where leaders want it to end up. A fourth is conversation about the business—that is, having an undirected exchange that yields various concerns, challenges, and opportunities.

1. Looking for Paradoxes That Reflect Fears and Values

The composite case study in Chapter 1 noted that ITHRes had teams in conflict that could readily articulate their values and fears, so that is what we focused on to surface some key paradoxes. One environment where this process would work is any company where teams have conflicting approaches to growth based on a skill focus versus a market focus. Another is an organization in a state of dramatic transition due to market changes or an acquisition.

For years, companies such as Right Management, Adecco, and Challenger, Gray & Christmas have had strong roots in career transition services. Prior to Web-based services becoming ubiquitous, these companies offered temporary office space, administrative support, and on-site screening and training services to employees that had been terminated by their client companies. At a very rapid pace, the need for the facilities decreased and employees in the career transition business saw their job descriptions morphing overnight. People who had spent their professional lives focused on helping others transition from one position or career to another suddenly found themselves with the same unsettling situation.

When I first came to Right Management, the annual global meetings had the character of celebrations, with a great sense of achievement and satisfaction related to steady growth. During the period when changes in the nature of the business were about to take hold firmly and quickly, the atmosphere changed. For some people, excitement swamped any fears they might have; for many others, fear of the changes dominated.

My background and leadership advisory experience were focused on the growth side of our customers' business, and I represented a new and developing arm of the business: organization consulting. Rather than respond to a client's need for services during an event like a layoff, those of us in the evolving part of the business anticipated clients' strategic needs and worked with companies to grow and to surpass their competition. We began to rely on paradox thinking as we sought to grow both parts of Right's business. Paradox thinking did not emerge out of deductive reasoning or years of dealing with tensions; it came out of the counter-cyclical nature of our clients' businesses. During tough years for our clients, their career transition needs increased. During profitable years, they had less need for Right Management. So even though our people knew that something had to change—we needed to start a new service, and as a result we embraced the paradox—at the same time some were fearful of a new model of operation. Concurrently, the desire to change came with a desire to uphold company values of service to clients. Much of the company's success in managing the paradox had to do with leadership getting on board with the shifts in direction and new demands on staff.

2. Parsing the Elements of a Chronic Struggle

An organization with a chronic challenge often just needs a little nudge and coaching to see its conflicting needs take shape. The senior executives at Georgia-Pacific clearly had just that when we began working together.

Georgia-Pacific is one of the world's leading manufacturers and marketers of tissue, packaging, paper, pulp, building products, and related chemicals. It employs nearly 35,000 people worldwide. New thinking about teaming and teamwork had triggered conversations about reorganization of work units. One struggle that bubbled up was that people on the shop floor in the Gypsum Division wanted to see things change, too, but as often occurs, resistance surfaced. A certain percentage of shop-floor employees were going to wait to adopt any changes until company leaders clarified the direction. What became apparent was that they couldn't just be reactive; shifts to improve efficiency or productivity had to reflect their thinking, too. In fact, they needed to take initiative. A balance of leadership and followership needed to extend to both executives and staff on the shop floor. And ultimately, it did.

3. Uncovering Paradoxes Inside of From-To Relationships

As noted in Chapter 1, Livli Hotels had gone from turning around its financial situation through cost controls and staff cutbacks to adopting a growth agenda. In discussing the implications of that with Liz P., the executive vice president for human resources, some paradoxes became evident. But when I got together with a team of nine leaders from HR, I introduced a from-to exercise to stimulate their thinking about conflicting pairs.

Following is the outcome of our conversation focused on HR value propositions. It's important to note that the intent was not to focus on how to move from what's in the left column to what's in the right. My intent in using this mechanism was specifically to surface paradoxes. The discussion that follows the table indicates what yielded paradoxes and what pointed clearly to either/or decisions.

From	To
Nice-to-have (yet, not priorities)	Staying focused on key priorities
More reactive with leaders	Proactive and strategic with leaders
Current level of leader hand-holding	Enabling leader ownership
80/20 push (even within HR)	80/20 pull (Livli Leadership Team, organization, HR)
Current pace as individuals	Faster as a team with priority focus
Current tools	More tools for capability building
Currently very good with operational excellence	Need to be competent in customer intimacy (and operational excellence is the ticket to admission); need to be innovative in service delivery
More focused on local	More focused on global
"Nice HR"	Good relationship with the ability to confront leaders

Arriving at the information in this table involved a conversation with the team members about what they individually and as a team felt were necessities. In some cases, what emerged was a decision that needed to be made on a specific step—an either/or; and in other cases, it was a need to create a balance with two interdependencies.

When they articulated those items, I posed this question: What do you have the most energy around? They zeroed in on "more focused on local" and "more focused on global." They began talking about them as "from" and "to" and, without any direction from me, what emerged was a clear sense that they needed to do both. The first paradox had emerged. The conversation naturally explored "What ifs": What would happen if we put all our focus on global and didn't pay attention to local? How is it possible to pay attention to the needs of local business units while we stay tuned in to what will give the company a stronger global presence?

A discussion tangentially related to the local-global discussion involves "current tools" and "more tools for capability building." In the list of current tools, they listed "expat," meaning the expatriate process, which they considered a tool both for developing high potential staff from different properties around the world and/or filling corporate needs for people with particular skills and talent. (Within the Livli system, the expat travels from a home country to another location where the company has facilities, typically for a period of one to three years. Often the person is filling a technical or leadership gap that cannot be filled locally, but while the person is in country, he or she will cultivate local talent as the ultimate permanent replacement.) Other current tools the company had to help build corporate capability included a talent planning process, succession program, and analytics. They all felt that those tools were fine, but not enough. The breadth of needs related to recruiting, hiring, screening, mentoring, evaluating, promoting, and so on would benefit from additional tools. And that led them to a "what" question: What tools do we need? As noted in this chapter, "what" questions often point to the need for an either/or approach. The cell within the table relating to tools, therefore, led to an either/or rather than a paradox.

Another conversation leading to the need for either/or thinking was moving from consideration of nice-to-haves to a clearer focus on priorities. Within the realm of priorities, however, the team could uncover paradoxes such as short-term needs *and* long-term needs. There was a similar layering in the concluding discussion about the human resources team being perceived as "a nice group," meaning that they are focused on the soft side of the organization. They are there to help, support, encourage, and so on, whereas other parts of the company are performance driven and focused on the bottom line. In doing those "hard" tasks, senior executives are not necessarily responsive to the "soft" needs, so HR needs to stand up to them. That is an either/or situation, but embedded in the concept of a more assertive HR team is the paradox of performance driven *and* relationship oriented.

The remaining discussions all surfaced paradoxes. In fact, with one exception, even their raw expression of the "from" and "to" captured interdependent opposites. The only one requiring a bit more explanation is the reference to 80/20. Within the HR team at Livli, the designation 80/20 refers to the way they talk about factors such as agreement and readiness. If they 80/20 agree on an idea, or are 80/20 ready to implement a plan, they consider that a win. When they take their idea or present their actions to senior executives, however, they feel they are nudging them much of the time. They want to move toward a situation where they are being invited more often to present ideas and take actions. The paradox emerging from this discussion could be called simply push *and* pull; another way of saying it is proactive *and* reactive.

4. Pulling Thematically From Conversation

Many of the 24 needs that emerged from my conversations related to Affirm Health's organizational challenges took on the veneer of either pro-facility or anti-facility, or pro-corporate or anti-corporate. That actually made it fairly easy to find pairs of conflicting needs.

In your own environment, consider the heated debates you have with team members or people from other departments as grand opportunities to discover pairs of conflicting needs within your organization. Someone in a senior position for facilities management might be parked on one side of a conference table across from a physician who is the CEO of a hospital. They would potentially have conflicts about where the money is spent and how best to support the mission of the company. In your situation, you might be someone in human resources arguing with finance, or a museum curator in conflict with an IT specialist. Disagreements such as these are precisely how you can unearth valuable paradoxes, so you don't have sit down to the conversation with the an attitude of "let's all get along." You just need to use the disagreement to walk away from the conversation with a sense that you're both on the same team, out to achieve the same Aim and avert the big Miss.

Here are the 12 pairings of conflicting needs for Affirm Health that came out of the conversations:

▶ Clinical needs *and* facilities needs—Without ever losing focus on quality patient care, there needs to be a coordinated effort to maintain structures in a first-class way.

▶ Reducing costs *and* increasing growth—The reality of reduced funds from key sources does not necessitate a hunker-down mentality when it comes to building the organization's talent, impact, and potential to serve more people.

▶ Slow, steady growth *and* agility—Pacing growth in consideration of resource constraints does not preclude moving quickly in some areas to keep up with changes in the environment and changing needs of constituents.

▶ Focus on today *and* preparation for tomorrow—Addressing immediate needs of patients and caregivers occurs concurrently with working toward realizing their long-range plan, which has the aim of providing access to care in all Affirm markets.

▶ Strategic plans *and* business plans—Vision and standards give an overarching sense of direction from headquarters while the individual hospitals keep their focus on day-to-day actions.

▶ Mission *and* margin—Staying true to a healing mission driven by compassion and dedication to care for those most in need requires money.

▶ Company standard *and* market brand—Carving out an identity in the marketplace and competing aggressively can only have sustained results if supported by consistency and excellence.

▶ Headquarters perspective *and* hospital perspective—Having a sense of operations being "our project" and "their project" builds synergy between headquarters and the individual facilities.

▶ Centralized control *and* distributed leadership—Individual hospital CEOs need the freedom to act on what they know is the best way to serve their populations; at the same time, it's important they adhere to best practices, budgets, and other corporate mandates.

▶ Nurturing relationship with managers/leaders *and* asserting expertise—Self/team-awareness of and confidence in skill areas must be coupled with an appropriate regard for authority.

▶ Master plan *and* responsiveness to needs—Sticking to the actions coming out of the strategic vision should not preclude making changes rapidly when necessary.

▶ Tight systems *and* flexibility in care—Efficiency and adherence to protocols at the service end combine with tweaking the rules and "staying loose" to deliver personalized and customized care.

Exercise: Identifying Paradoxes in Your Organization

The process of identifying paradoxes is a process of simplification. You may start with a sense that your organization has an overwhelming number of problems and concerns, only to find that you can distill all of them down to two or three categories of needs.

1. Throw all the issues on the table.
2. Put them into pairs of conflicting needs.
3. Group those pairs thematically.

This three-step exercise is the first of four woven through the upcoming chapters.

With Affirm's 12 pairs, step three—grouping the pairs thematically—took shape this way:

Short Term and Long Term

Focus on today *and* preparation for tomorrow.

Business plans *and* strategic plans.

Reducing costs *and* increasing growth.

Slow, steady growth *and* agility.

Control and Freedom

Tight systems *and* flexibility in care.

Master plan *and* responsiveness to needs.

Headquarters perspective *and* hospital perspective.

Company standard *and* market brand.

Centralized control *and* distributed leadership.

Nurturing relationship with managers/leaders *and* asserting expertise.

Why and How

Mission *and* margin.

Clinical needs *and* facility needs.

Stacking does not always suggest that there is a compounded effect to the downside, but it is often the result that occurs. In a set of stacked paradoxes, over-focus on one side means you are managing to the downside of multiple paradoxes. In the Affirm example, consider the stacked paradoxes grouped thematically under "short term and long term." They are the top three in the list:

Focus on today *and* preparation for tomorrow.

Business plans *and* strategic plans.

Reducing costs *and* increasing growth.

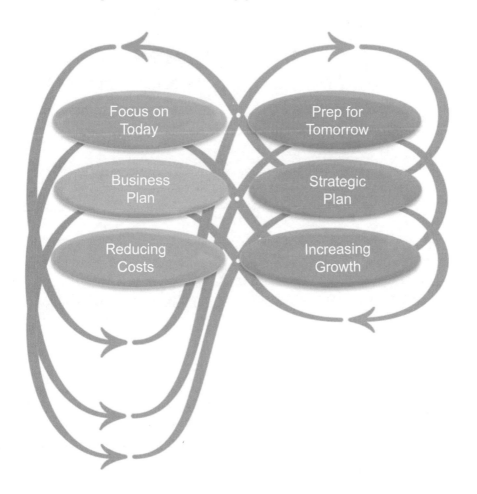

There is a possibility of being pulled to the downside on either side, but more commonly, in the case of pairs grouped as "short term and long term," it's over-focus on the short term that occurs and leads to an imbalance. Organizations simply tend to put more pressure on achieving short-term goals. The deadlines are tighter, and the evaluations occur more frequently.

The fourth paradox listed under the theme "short term and long term" is "slow steady growth *and* agility," and it is not stacked with the others. Rather, it is nested inside the Increasing Growth pole.

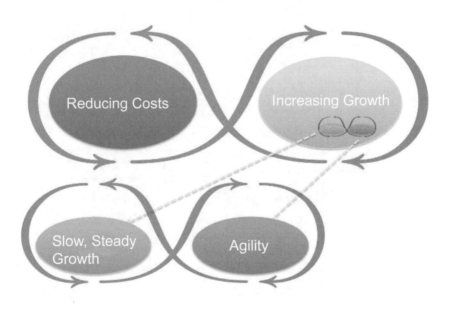

The practical value of visually representing the relationships in this manner receives attention in the upcoming chapters on mapping positive and negative outcomes, action steps, and metrics. In brief, mapping can give you an immediate picture of whether you're headed for success or have inadvertently created some big problems for yourself and your organization.

Evaluating When Paradox Thinking Is Necessary

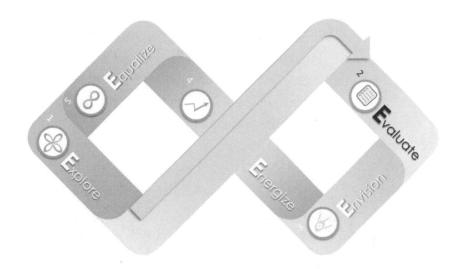

There are situations in which paradox thinking is exactly what you need, and then there are times when you need to decide between options. Now that you have begun identifying paradoxes in your organization, let's step back and explore when you need to manage them and when you need to determine that only one option is viable.

Many environments engender and reward either/or thinking; in fact, people in leadership roles often associate that false dichotomy with confidence and success. A colonel decides to send troops to one location rather than another for a surprise attack. A football coach chooses between Play A and Play B to win the game. A doctor relies on quick either/or thinking to make a life-or-death decision. In situations like these, choosing one possibility over another may be necessary to solve a problem.

The decision-maker who seems decisive earns admiration as long as most of the decisions lead to good outcomes. The pressure on individuals, team leaders, and senior executives to make decisions quickly, to zero in on the better option—spotting the advantages of one over another—is intense. Those who ponder too long can put their jobs at risk.

However, much to the detriment of all kinds of organizations, this mentality has led to either/or decision-making as the default approach instead of one that's consciously chosen because it fits the circumstances. Ironically, either/or decisions—which are often necessary—come more easily and are better informed when coming out of the context of both/and thinking.

The colonel, coach, and doctor have limited ability to replicate their success if they lack the foundation of both/and thinking. Without being able to consider the both/and model, they could find themselves relying on fallible intuition and an uneven ability to analyze situations quickly. They all face strategic tensions prior to making problem-solving decisions. When they recognize what those tensions are and the needs on which they are based, the choices they may have to make down the road can be informed decisions. For the colonel, those conflicting needs might be troop strength _and_ high-tech weaponry. The coach could be faced with the prospects of luring a star quarterback _and_ a handful of solid, mid-level players. For the doctor, it might be long-term therapy _and_ a surgical quick-fix. Focusing on such interdependent pairs is generally not an intuitive thing. It's a learned process.

In looking at Affirm Health's two dozen conflicting needs that came out of my conversations, the first pair to take shape was "clinical needs _and_ facilities needs." An isolated focus on the requirements for providing superior care means that elevators might break down. Making the needs of facilities the priority means that Affirm could build the wrong building very well.

Reviewing highlights of the conversations that were related to the conflict between clinical and facilities needs steered us directly into the path of the either/or questions to emerge from the pair. Hospital CEOs are often doctors, so the challenge of caring for buildings often strikes them as secondary to patient care. Using patch solutions to address facilities issues can seem acceptable. A focus on facilities needs means making sure the structure is well maintained, but from their perspective, this could come at the expense of having the resources necessary for good clinical care. The CEOs needed headquarters' executives to identify both a threshold and a cap on the dollars that the CEO could spend for facilities and should spend on facilities.

The Facilities Resource Group had some control over how that money is spent, but each individual CEO had control as well, with no clear line of demarcation indicating where that authority ended. And because there was such a heavily distributed leadership model, the head of that group had a difficult or even impossible time finding out what kind of money was being spent. He also needed to grasp when there was an intimate relationship between facilities upkeep and patient care—for example, the riskiness of the electrical system failing for five seconds.

Either/or questions—the answers to which had to be informed by looking at clinical needs and facilities needs as a pair of interdependent opposites—include the following:

- What is the maximum amount a given hospital CEO can spend annually on the facility?
- What is the reporting structure for facilities expenditures?
- When must reports be filed?
- Who receives the reports?
- When will the facility be inspected?
- Who from the hospital interfaces with the Facilities Resource Group?

Out of this short list, an interesting pattern emerged. I will not call this a "rule of either/or," but rather a hint at how you might determine either/or questions. None of these questions begins with the interrogative "why" or "how." They are who, what, when, and where questions. You will find that often—not always, but often—these are the types of questions that involve either/or decision-making.

The conversation with Liz P. at Livli Hotels that launched our exploration of the company's goals and paradoxes began with a few "what" questions. What was wrong with the structure that it took so long to do certain things? What kind of compensation approach could be configured that would elicit acceptance from both headquarters and the individual general managers? The "whats" were like road markers on our quick trip toward discovering the Livli paradox of global *and* local.

The reason that who, what, when, and where are often associated with either/or thinking is that they often signal needs that are framed by time. "When must the reports be filed?" is not an ongoing issue. It is decided, and then whoever decided it moves on to the next problem. Even budgeting is not an ongoing issue; rather, it's a recurring one.

The core distinction in deciding when to use either/or and when to use both/and is that the former type of thinking serves those acute problems well, whereas both/and thinking is required for chronic challenges and issues.

Either/Or in Planning

Although they do not use the same vocabulary or models as I do, authors Michael E. Raynor and Mumtaz Ahmed spotlight the vital need to embrace key interdependent opposites in their work on the rules for corporate success. Their article, "Three Rules for Making a Company Truly Great," which appeared in the *Harvard Business Review* (April 2013), spells out these principles:

> "1. Better before cheaper—compete on differentiators other than price.

2. Revenue before costs—make increasing revenues a priority over reducing costs; in other words, you cannot cut your way to growth.

3. There are no other rules—so change whatever you must to follow rules 1 and 2.[1]"

If I've succeeded in getting you to shift a bit toward both/and thinking, you may be reading these principles and concluding, "They can't be interdependent opposites; there's no 'and'"! In fact, the phraseology merely implies an important point in dealing with such pairs: Interdependent opposites are not always equally weighted. They both receive attention, but one may receive more emphasis. When a company is transforming, senior leadership will naturally put more emphasis on change rather than staying stable. At the same time, the leaders can't afford to lose sight of maintaining stability or the changes could take them off course.

For example, the rule "better before cheaper" doesn't mean that a company should ignore what a product costs; price needs to be managed as well as quality. But when a company breaks the rule, it ends up like Acer, which announced in 2011 that it would try to return to profitability by no longer making "cheap junk."[2] The concept of managing to the upside is relevant to this discussion, and I'll illustrate how giving more weight to one part of the pair does not mean you can't manage to the upside of the other one. See Chapter 5 for more on this topic.

When I first saw the title of the article by Raynor and Ahmed, I immediately wanted to see what was missing. Typically, if odd numbers of goals, objectives, or principles suggest that something might be missing—that is, that one side of a pair has been ignored—that's a red flag for me. For example, in one of the meetings with the Livli Hotels team, we made a list of their ground rules and plugged them into the opposite sides of infinity loops. One of the rules—"simple"—was not part of a pair. When they thought through it, they determined that the concept of "comprehensive" was missing. In the case of "the three rules" (also the title of Raynor's and Ahmed's new book), there are really only two rules, with the third being an admonition to follow the first two.

The article doesn't stop with these two rules representing both/ and thinking. It goes on to state the following: "With few exceptions the best companies behave as though these principles guide them through all their important decisions, from acquisitions to divestitures to resource allocation to pricing."[3] In other words, the principles guide them toward either/or decisions. You can't make informed choices about those other issues unless you have the foundation of knowing what the choices come of out—and those are the interdependent relationships of quality/price and revenue/cost-constraints.

Although either/or thinking does not necessarily lead to an action, it might be a critical part of an evaluation process that precedes an action. Consider the growth possibilities faced by ITHRes, the composite company introduced in Chapter 1. To support its assertion that growth could come from partnering with a company specializing in moving businesses, the sales and marketing team had to take an either/ or approach in forming selection criteria. There were no action-oriented decisions involved—the company was still just thinking about how to proceed—but the team had to go through the exercise of setting up a profile of an ideal partner; otherwise their proposal would seem too nebulous. And that meant making choices.

Sales and marketing ultimately concluded that an ideal partner would meet the following criteria:

- It operated with a scalable model, using contractors regularly, _rather than_ one that usually deployed its own staff to do a job.
- In all likelihood, a company with years of experience would be _better than_ a young or startup company that had not yet established a track record.

▶ The company should have a "get it right the first time" mentality, like ITHRes, *versus* "if it breaks, we'll come back and fix it."

Armed with this profile, the teams discussing the options for growth discovered an interesting irony. The technical team realized that their ideal target client for IT education and consulting would essentially be the opposite kind of company from the one favored by sales and marketing. They would be better off with a company that wanted to upgrade the skills and systems of a stable workforce. A young company might see ITHRes as able to help it get a running start. And it would be good for continuing business if that company had an appreciation that the IT department would benefit from ongoing upgrades and fixes.

Using the tool of either/or thinking in this manner actually brought the two teams closer to an understanding of how pursuit of both growth options might balance their portfolio of business relationships. "And" suddenly seemed like a desirable path.

The move from paradox thinking to action means you will be setting priorities, so you will put either/or thinking to work as well. Either/or and both/and do not function in isolation, therefore. They are both necessary; they help each other.

Both/And as a Complement to Either/Or

One executive told me about a merger that tanked, and he did not catch the downward plunge in time. This is someone I consider very intuitive, and he admitted that he had sensed how ill-fated the venture was at a critical point. But he took no action. Why? Even considering that the merger started to turn sour, his reputation as a decision-maker—his prowess in using logic and analysis to make a decision—was at stake. He had wrapped himself in either/or.

Each of the various decision-makers in this scenario began with a drive toward growth and a commitment to the status quo—stability—in terms of principles of client service. Growth and stability were the joint forces that drove them toward a merger in the first place. Immediately after recognizing that their goals meshed, they proceeded with plans to merge. Given that they shared an overarching paradox of growth _and_ stability, they initiated merger proceedings.

Their next focus was a set of either/or decisions that included:

- Where should they make their headquarters after merging with another firm?
- When should they make the move?
- What would the structure of the new firm be?
- Who would staff the different locations?
- What would the performance goals of the firm be?
- What would people at the different levels be paid?

Consumed by answering those questions, they failed to pay attention to corporate culture. It is quite possible to merge two organizations in perfect harmony on paper, but when the element of human habits, values, assumptions, and priorities—that is, the characteristics of a corporate culture—come into play, the merger can become a toxic stew.

We tend to have a disposition to stick by the either/or decisions we make. That supposed virtue of being decisive involves building defenses around decision-making. One of the greatest values of using paradox as a conceptual model for approaching issues is that such either/or decisions can be quickly reexamined in the context of the whole picture.

Let's say the executive responded to his gut feeling, and took a moment to step back and look at the "why" of the merger. The firm wanted growth _and_ stability (so did the other firm). One of the steps that had the potential to promote growth was a merger. At that junction, the either/or decision of "to merge or not to merge" came into play. Did he (and his counterpart in the other firm) then lose sight of stability as a paradoxical goal? A fundamental element of stability in both organizations was their unique culture; it's what made them productive and high-functioning organisms. In re-examining the decision-making process, the executive I was meeting with might have realized—before it was too late—that his push for growth jeopardized stability. He could have backed away from the merger with a sense of being proactive rather than being "wrong" about targeting that particular firm for the merger.

As I said earlier, the process of using paradox thinking can be counterintuitive. It doesn't negate the value of intuition; however, it does balance it.

It's only fair to point out that, even when an either/or decision-making process is informed by a grasp of the underlying paradoxes, that doesn't necessarily produce a positive outcome. Human beings are creatures capable of infinite optimism and pessimism, of great logic and nonsense; in short, we embody paradox. We may, therefore, go into a meeting with the intent of closing a deal based on informed choices and end up walking out of the meeting with an abhorrence of the deal. Such was the case with the company in this scenario.

Executives from my client company entered negotiations for a potential merger with an appreciation for three underlying paradoxes:

- Cost-constraints *and* growth in revenue.
- The other company's culture *and* the acquiring company's culture.
- Global growth *and* local growth.

The executives left the meeting in a state of conflict. Some thought the deal should proceed, and some thought it should be aborted. Substantial opportunities (or losses) were at stake. This was a move that would either take the company into a digital services business in a big way or keep them looking for another portal into e-commerce.

They'd had an ethos that throwing resources into an idea would allow it to grow. They wanted to support further innovation. Some of the executives of the first company felt a clash of cultures; they didn't see the "and" anymore; they were American cowboys with a spirit of adventure. The company they wanted to acquire had an "old world" mentality, in their opinion. That company thought their technological innovation was mature and no further change was necessary at the moment. In their opinion, the idea didn't need to grow; it needed to be taken to market.

So the two companies came to the date knowing why they *should* marry—based on the paradoxes—and left in conflict because feelings and intuition superseded reason. Again, using paradox thinking is often counterintuitive. Paradox thinking is important supplemental thinking that needs to be balanced with gut reactions, which tend to be rooted in either/or thinking.

When Paradox Thinking Is Necessary

And, of course, in any number of circumstances, paradox thinking isn't just the desirable path; it's the necessary one.

In their book, *The Three Tensions: Winning the Struggle to Perform without Compromise*, Dominic Dodd and Ken Favaro argue that a requirement for consistent success is achieving both goals of these three tensions:

1. Profitability—growth.
2. Results today—results tomorrow.
3. The performance of the company as a whole—the performance of its individual parts.

They then expose a novel way of rating a company's track record in achieving that balance. They call it a batting average, based on the formula used in baseball. "The batting average is a measure of how often a business achieves both of the two objectives at the same time within a given tension."[4] And whereas hitting .300 in baseball represents solid performance, the standard for a successful company is .500. Dodd and Favaro assert that is the rate of the companies in the top quartile of shareholder return.

Based on their research, which included data from executives at 200 companies around the world as well as analysis of the performance of hundreds of other companies, the authors document what I have seen time after time in my consulting practice: Most companies swing from an emphasis on one part of an interdependent pair to a focus on the other. Unless they're coached to do it, they don't try to achieve both at the same time. *The Three Tensions* quantifies the assertion:

▶ In the surveys the authors conducted with executives, roughly 60 percent of their companies chose either profit or growth at any given time, but not both.

▶ About 70 percent either went for current performance over building for tomorrow, or did the reverse.

▶ About 70 percent also emphasized the parts over the whole, or vice versa.[5]

But the real value of the research provided by Dodd and Favaro is in their quantifying the success of the companies that batted .500 and the failure of those with a zero batting average. Again, it's exactly the kind of results I've seen when companies exploit the energy of interdependent opposites in their organizations. Probably the most striking, general conclusion to come out of their work is how closely a company's batting average is tied to its total shareholder return (the measure of the performance of stocks and shares over time). In other words, the better a company managed the three tensions, the higher its total return. That is a compelling, bottom-line argument in favor of using a paradox approach.

Another illustration of the value and necessity of using both/and thinking comes from companies dealing with government regulation that impacts their day-to-day operations. To varying degrees, all companies need to comply with government regulations, even if they pertain only to taxes. Companies that face a mountain of regulations that concern safety, health, energy, and/or other factors often have a complex relationship with the government that forces them into both/ and thinking. They find some regulation desirable; from a marketing perspective, being in compliance with tough government standards engenders consumer trust. On the other hand, too much regulation constrains their capability to innovate and generate profit. The gene-sis of the ENERGY STAR program reflects the come-hither/go-away relationship that the high-tech industry was forced to cultivate with government in the early 1990s.

Toward the end of President Clinton's first term, the Environmental Protection Agency (EPA) and the Department of Energy (DOE) decided to do something to get industries to produce energy-efficient products. Early on, they directed their attention to the computer industry, which promptly had their representatives sit down at the table with EPA and DOE personnel to carve out a voluntary program. Concurrently, many lobbyists for the computer industry stayed on the "go-away" side of the equation, doing what they could to ensure that a scheme for voluntary compliance did not morph into a regulatory mandate. If the industry had taken an either/or approach to the government initiative, it could have been a winner-take-all proposition: Either regulations would go into effect or industry would force the "green people" in the Clinton administration to back down. Neither of those scenarios represents an ideal outcome for the people who were not even involved: consumers.

People with any measure of leadership responsibility need to find a balance of interdependent opposites. A classroom teacher knows that memorization and reciting facts have a place in learning, but empha-sizing rote learning at the expense of cognitive development keeps stu-dents from reaching their full potential. Executives can similarly hold their companies back, committing all of their resources to one possi-bility without adequately considering the possibilities represented by its interdependent opposite. Decisions emerging from intuition, spot analysis, or some idiosyncratic type of logic tend to swing the pendulum in one direction only. That either/or approach—that committed lack of balance—means that the organization can expect a mighty swing back in the other direction.

Chapter 4

The Importance of Leaders at All Levels

"Leadership is action, not position."
—John C. Maxwell

As an individual, you may find it very easy to absorb and use paradox thinking to shine in problem-solving, both as a personal and a career development tool. When it comes to integrating paradox thinking into company-wide strategic planning and operations, however, there is strength in numbers. No matter where you sit in the organizational hierarchy, you can lead those around you to an awareness of the power of "and." Essentially, you add "change leader" to your job description.

In this chapter, I feature approaches to leading such change, which is potentially dramatic. If your organization's culture has always functioned with a guiding principle of "which option is better" or "there's a right and a wrong," then the mere possibility that conflicting needs might be addressed with equal weight and resources sounds countercultural. Yet, paradox thinking will distinguish you as a business-minded, innovative thinker in that same organization.

This chapter also includes profiles of executives I work with who faced the challenge of inculcating entire organizations with an appreciation for paradox thinking. They affected the organization's ability to manage major objectives that appeared to be at odds. And the most pronounced dual result of their success: organizations with impressive profit margins that also happened to be great places to work. In other words, the leaders featured here engendered high, individual performance and a strong sense of teamwork.

Paths to Change Leadership

There are multiple ways to describe the process of leading change in an organization. Start by using Maslow's Hierarchy to enhance your understanding of why people can have so much emotion about taking a new path. In the hierarchy of needs described by psychologist Abraham Maslow, people have to have a lower tier of needs met before they can address those at a higher level.

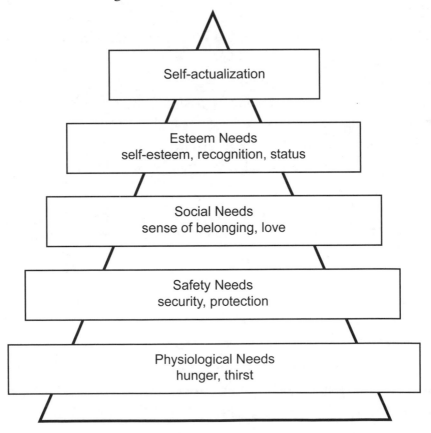

When looking at change, people in an organization may feel that their work life is all about connecting with colleagues and moving up the ladder to distinguish themselves. Suddenly, someone at the senior level announces a change. Consciously or subconsciously, they might find that they are questioning their safety needs—job security, where they will be physically located to do their job, and so on. If you've ever rescued an animal and brought it into a new environment, you can better understand the mentality of some people in facing change in the workplace. There is fear of the unknown, even though there might be some optimism that change could represent something positive. For some in the midst of workplace change, it represents amazing opportunities for thriving; for those who are change averse, it feels like the fight for survival will increase in intensity.

The fear response—fight, flight, or freeze—can come into play to varying degrees during a period of workplace change. Some will resist strongly and offer what they believe are compelling reasons why status quo should prevail. Others will look for a way out. Still others will seem to be paralyzed; they need to be ushered to "safety."

And the fact is, people are very different in their determination of what constitutes meaningful or dramatic change. Case in point: Implementing a new user interface for an online database will upset some people for weeks.

In his book, *Rangers Lead the Way: The Army Rangers' Guide to Leading Your Organization Through Chaos*, former Army Ranger Dean Hohl has a simple model for explaining how people move through change. Hohl uses experiential learning modeled on Ranger training, such as four days of combat training in the woods of Kentucky, to drive home the process. At first, some people are in state of denial: "This can't be happening!" The next thing they do is resist: "No way will this work!" With insightful leadership such as listening to the wisdom in resistance and involving others along the way, people next begin to explore what the change represents. And then in response to what they have heard, and through setting an example to show their own partici-pation in change, effective leaders help them to commit to the change.

The value of Hohl's analysis in examining organizational change is that the latter happens on a person-by-person basis. Whether the num-ber of individuals affected is a handful or thousands, each one moves through some kind of process before arriving at commitment.

A graphic representation of the transformation in thinking and behavior is as follows:

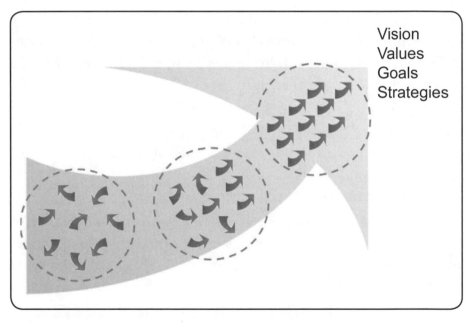

The arrow graphic is illuminating. When I use it to describe what appears to be dysfunction in an organization as represented by the arrows going in all different directions, people immediately get it. They understand that there are individuals and/or teams wanting to do the right thing—to work toward a common goal. Yet without alignment toward the overall vision, values, goals, and strategies of the organi-zation, the gears aren't turning together. Those in formal leadership roles need to lead change proactively, not simply express what needs to happen. When there is greater clarity about the direction the organization needs to move in, arrows start to line up around the leaders.

I was working with a global, mid-sized specialty chemical company experiencing management conflicts while they were going through an enterprise resource planning (ERP) implementation. They were upgrading systems throughout the organization to make their operations current, vis-à-vis the rest of the industry. At that point, they had spent millions of dollars and had some false starts relative to the ERP effort.

I conducted individual interviews with everyone on the senior team to get a deeper sense of the conflict. That gave me what I needed to help the CEO see why there were costly false starts. Individuals weren't connecting the dots about the changes. They didn't have a cohesive, big picture about how the changes were interrelated. The diagram helped everyone put words to what they were experiencing; they understood that they had not been lining up in the same direction as the CEO.

With people now aware that dysfunction existed in the organization, the CEO got clarity on his task. He needed to articulate how the changes supported the company's vision, values, goals, and strategy. He had to be explicit about the way people needed to sync up, and then show what steps had already been taken in that direction.

Using the diagram does not stop with awareness, however. It is useful in helping to structure discussions on sequencing. With this organization—first in small groups and then in larger ones—we labeled the arrows; they became different teams and initiatives. By going through this exercise, it was easy to see who and what would start to turn around in response to movement by another "arrow." In this case, the work of realigning was a focused, two-day effort that succeeded in helping to engage leadership and engage others throughout the organization in moving toward the stated vision, values, goals, and strategy.

Organizational Change Process Strategy

A number of years ago, I developed a change process wherein an organization's leaders come together in order to accomplish three objectives:

1. Focus on creating their desired future.
2. Align their extended leadership team.
3. Engage the entire organization in focusing on the future and delivery of business priorities.

The change process becomes a framework providing guidance, helping leaders instill flexibility in the thinking and behavior of people involved in the change. They then become the change mechanism. In doing so, they move through the cycle of personal change from denial to commitment. I later saw that some of the steps complemented elements of John Kotter's highly regarded 8-Step Process for Leading Change.[1]

As you go through my steps, keep in mind that the underlying premise is that you rely on a change process that recognizes paradox—that is, you want to change *and* recognize the value in what you are doing currently. To use a cliché, in the process of changing, you don't want to throw the baby out with the bath water. Throughout the change process, another paradox must be embedded: focus on today *and* focus on tomorrow.

1. **Baseline current behavior.** In terms of their perception of change—good or bad—entire departments can vary a great deal, not just individuals. Whether your focus is a project team of six or a company of 6,000, begin by assessing the readiness for change. For example, your team may want to shut the door on a method of thinking that gives equal weight to two opposing courses of action, such as "innovate *and* improve existing technology." Or, you may be working with people who jump at the chance to incorporate new thinking that may give them an edge in achieving team and corporate goals. What you ascertain about their readiness for change shapes your next step.

2. **Develop a compelling case for change.** If you have people in your organization whose feet are planted in resistance, then articulate a case for change. A "compelling case" lays out the potential benefits of change for the individuals involved and the organization. It expresses the value and importance of the change, but it isn't like a smoke alarm going off. A "sense of urgency" captures reasons why immediate action must happen. It is the proverbial wakeup call.

3. **Set an example.** If you don't change, why would anybody else? In order to sell the case for paradox thinking to management, colleagues, and/or staff, a leader needs to demonstrate that it has utility in his or her own professional life. As a reminder that leaders occur at every level, I want to share the story of a friend of mine who was a part-time administrative assistant when this occurred. She had gone to a weekend seminar on interpersonal communication and picked up what she thought were brilliant ways of sorting information. In a full staff meeting at the trade association where she worked, she was one of 35 people sitting around a couple of conference tables that had been shoved together. The person next to her was one of the senior leaders and she started talking about breakdowns in interdepartmental communication. My friend privately offered her the insights on communication she had learned the previous weekend. The executive who had the concern discovered more about the approach described by my friend and started using it. The following month at the staff meeting, she shared what she'd learned and how she tried to put it into practice; other department heads at the table concurred that her new way of addressing written and verbal communication seemed to be an improvement. The executive director of the organization not only nodded in agreement, but also led the entire organization in revamping policies on memos, phone communication, e-mails, and so on. All my friend did was say, "Here's what I learned" to someone who could lead by example. This is the best way to create awareness of the value of change.

4. **Refocus work.** One of the simplest ways to exploit the opportunities associated with paradox thinking is to incorporate it into work processes. The upcoming chapters give you practical tools to make that happen. The intent is to see the mental picture of potential benefits come alive. In Kotter's terms, it would be all about "communicating a vision for buy-in."[2] This is where talk takes shape in the form of tables, graphs, action plans, and checklists. In Dean Hohl's schema, it's where change-averse people go from resistance to exploration.

5. **Advance skills and knowledge.** In many cases, when people are asked to work differently from the way they did previously, they lack confidence in how to do it. You might consider having an informal workshop where there's no pressure to perform, yet the context of the workshop and specific activities enable people to feel free in trying new things. It's a great way to lead them all the way into the exploration phase of change and give them the opportunity to do some skill-building with the models used to support paradox thinking. Try to incorporate mentoring into the program as well so there is on-the-job learning without intimidation.

6. **Generate short-term wins.** This step correlates with John Kotter's process, but to make it applicable here, we need clarity on what constitutes a "win." Wins reflect progress, some visible, positive difference connected with the change. A short-term win could be moving the location of staff meetings around so that people in different parts of the organization feel more connected to it. Eliminating a report that didn't provide much information yet took precious time to complete is a win.

7. **Renew the energy.** Change isn't a one-time thing. The change in the way you and your organization approach innovation, as well as think through problems and solve them, evolves into the new normal or business as usual. That's a reflection of having reached the commitment phase of change. At the

same time, it's important to keep energy high about the value of the change. Leaders can do this by helping people take stock and celebrate the victories, including failures that were averted. Chapter 7 of the book looks at how metrics figure into the process of applying paradox thinking; they are a great tool to help leaders talk about positive outcomes both qualitatively and quantitatively.

8. **Integrate the change into the culture.** When a paradox approach to challenges and opportunities becomes "how we do things here," then employees are mentored in it, just as they learn the other policies and principles that characterize the organization. The culture itself is thereby enriched with new performance advantage. It results in a source of pride and distinction.

Robert ("Jake") Jacobs looks at the change process somewhat differently. First, he advocates an immersion approach, which he describes in *Real-Time Strategic Change: How to Involve an Entire Organization in Fast and Far-Reaching Change.* He believes in involving everyone in an organization in the change process at the same time. Second, he embeds the use of paradox—he calls it polarity—thinking. He focuses on having everyone in an organization viewing change in terms of interdependent opposites. Those he cites as key are:

▶ Inquiring about what others believe *and* advocating for what you believe.

▶ Planning for your future *and* being in your future now.

▶ The organization achieving its full potential *and* people achieving their full potential.

▶ Knowing the inside of your organization *and* knowing the outside of your organization.

▶ Providing direction *and* inviting participation.

▶ Combining the best of your past and present *and* envisioning compelling future possibilities.[3]

Putting Paradox Into Practice in Leading Change

The individuals featured in this section made important choices that reflect paradox thinking. All occupy senior level positions in their organizations. That gave them the ability, if they chose to exercise it, to dictate change in an "I say, you do" style. Instead, they chose to involve others and value the diversity of thinking around them. They also focused on a set of seemingly opposite goals that were central to the organization's sustainability.

In organizations where a senior executive imposes change rather than leads it, the arrows may still line up, but only for the short term. The change is not without coercion and attrition. Instead of people within the organization helping to engender acceptance and enthusiasm for a new approach in a contagious way, they do what they're told, with a number of people choosing to leave or being terminated.

World Wide Technology CEO Jim Kavanaugh is all about balance; paradox thinking comes naturally to him. When it looked as though World Wide Technology might not make it, his joint focus on cost constraints and investment in growth turned the company around. During its first few years of life, the company was mired in debt, having accumulated $2 million in debt within three years. Kavanaugh blamed it on "poor financial discipline."[4] While addressing that and reining in expenses, he set out to use any available cash to reinvest back into his people, culture, services, and solutions: "It's been a conscious strategy to build products internally on our nickel with the intent to make them robust enough to sell to the commercial marketplace."[5]

The plan to pursue seemingly opposing goals concurrently worked. The company has $5 billion in annual sales and employs 2,200 people in offices around the globe. World Wide Technology is known not only for its profitable growth—25 percent year-over-year growth for the last 15 years—but also for being a great place to work. In this area of performance, the company once again scored a national ranking: World Wide Technology is ranked #24 on *Fortune*'s "100 Best Companies to

Work For" list. The company's values are very important, and people throughout the organization are expected to live up to them. In fact, those values are so central to what Kavanaugh and his leadership team have built that the latter's position description on the company Website states: "Jim currently focuses his time in the areas of long term planning, financial performance, employee development, and WWT's continued adherence to its core value system."[6]

The company embraces core principles such as "no surprises," and "face the facts." Some of the language was inspired by Jim Collins's *Good to Great,* but Kavanaugh and other senior executives at World Wide Technology demonstrate the concepts and integrated the language.

In one meeting, Kavanaugh specified that the balance he's always been focused on is performance *and* culture, meaning a high standard of individual performance *and* a culture of collaboration and cooperation—that is, a team mindset. Adherence to the company's core values facilitates accomplishing both: No matter whether a person is operating individually or in the context of a team, those values guide the actions.

Harlan Kent, CEO of Yankee Candle, has faced a similar set of choices that Jim Kavanaugh did during the turnaround period. That is, he wants concurrently to hold down expenses while investing in growth. It's a balancing act that has resulted in impressive resilience: Unlike many companies driven to layoffs by the recession that began in 2008, Yankee Candle opened more than 30 stores a year and created new jobs.

Yankee Candle's core business is itself a paradox. Widely known for its high-quality, fragrant candles, it has also brought consumers new fragrances. Yankee Candle is therefore a business that infuses wax (and other substances) with fragrance and a business that develops fragrances that can be used in multiple delivery systems. The tagline often appearing in conjunction with the company name captures the paradox well: Yankee Candle Company—A Passion for Fragrance.

There is another "and" embedded in Kent's success story. Focusing too much on cost containment has the potential to drive down entrepreneurial spirit—the lifeblood of consumer goods business like this—because it would be seen as embodying too much risk. Balancing his efforts to drive down expenses is his continuing support of a culture that has encouraged breaking out in new directions.

Kent himself took a risk to prove that he was open to new ideas to solve problems and find new creative paths. For the television show *Undercover Boss*, he disguised himself as an entry-level employee in four roles: sales associate, packer, store manager, and second assistant manager. He made discoveries about when and how not to cut costs, what kind of leadership talent resided in someone who packed boxes of candles for the company, and much more. Such executive exposure to people who make the company hum on a daily basis is very likely to make it clearer how doing this *and* that—in this case, cost containment *and* growth—can be an achievable paradox that can engage employees at all levels.

Ron Levy, former CEO of SSM Health Care–St. Louis Network, crowned a series of leadership challenges with an impressive turnaround at the St. Louis Network. To achieve this meant having everybody on the same page with a robust, or even passionate, commitment to change. A $3 billion a year not-for-profit healthcare company, with SSM-St. Louis Network responsible for over half of the revenues, SSM Health Care System was the first in its industry to win the Malcolm Baldridge National Quality Award, a prestigious award named after the secretary of commerce under President Ronald Reagan.

When I first sat down with Levy, I asked, "What is it that's made you effective in turning around so many healthcare organizations? What is it about your leadership and about your approach to turnaround?"

Levy began with his back-to-basics philosophy that immediately addressed the need to stay focused on fulfilling the organization's care-giving mission *and* improving margins at the same time. At the St. Louis Network, for example, it was critical to get key stakeholders, physicians, and staff, across their seven hospitals, not only to continue to provide exceptional patient care, but also to rise to the challenge that there needed to be a new approach to care delivery and a new direction for the organization. Very simply, making service improvements for physicians and patients, and the emphasis on excellent care, led to increases in the number of patients served and market share, from 14.8 percent to just more than 20 percent. Combined with cost-reduction measures, the result was that the St. Louis Network logged a nearly $30 million profit in 2002, which represents a $50 million turnaround since Levy took over in 1999. Not coincidentally, 2002 was the year the SSM Health Care System won the Baldridge Quality Award.

This was essentially his approach with the other healthcare organizations where he and his teams effected turnarounds. His leadership at SSM's St. Clare Hospital in Wisconsin in the 1980s took the 100-bed hospital from a negative operating margin to a 4-to-6-percent margin while creating a rural system of healthcare delivery for the surrounding area. In the early 1990s, he raised operating margins to about 5.5 percent at SSM's St. Mary's Health Center in St. Louis. Subsequently, he had similar success at the St. Louis Network and the newly formed physicians' organization, where he and his team were able to reduce the group's operating losses by more than 50 percent. Through the years colleagues have noted Levy's dual emphasis on margin and mission, not simply focusing on finance, but also on improvements in quality and service in everything they do. Levy attributes this success to building a cohesive team, all pulling in the same direction, and getting stakeholders involved on Day One.

Levy knew financial performance could only do so much, so he leveraged the fact that people who worked in the healthcare professions of St. Louis Network felt intimately tied to the mission of SSM Health Care System: "Through our exceptional health care services, we reveal the healing presence of God."[7] Perhaps one of the most compelling pieces of evidence that SSM staff bought into the mission statement is that it was developed with input from nearly 3,000 employees.

In sizing up the situation, Levy also saw another important pair of interdependent opposites: people *and* process. One immediate impact of focusing on that paradox was a sense of how strongly personal missions and the corporate mission aligned. Employee engagement comes out of this kind of alignment; people have an easier time dealing with process changes when they feel that personal affiliation to a higher purpose and they actively participate in the organizational change.

Levy set out to effect a transformation. Step one was taking the long view and setting the strategy. Step two was creating a team at the St. Louis Network to help lead implementation. Step three was engaging physicians and other staff network-wide in the goals of the organization and buying into the idea that change that was necessary for long-term financial sustainability and success. It involved, as he said, "a lot of messaging—a lot of communication."[8] Even when people agree that change is a good idea, implementation becomes difficult at some point. It's all part of teambuilding, strategy, execution, and repositioning—of helping people see and understand the facts and the challenges before them related to the change.

To conclude the profiles on leaders who effected key changes organization-wide, I am highlighting Greig Woodring, briefly referenced in Chapter 1. When Reinsurance Group of America (RGA) experienced major structural changes in 2008 and then again 2011, new leadership paradoxes took shape for Woodring as CEO. The company's transition to a matrix organization in 2011 meant he was leading the movement toward more integrated systems instead of a loosely affiliated group of reinsurance companies. Centralizing processes too much—exercising an excessive amount of executive control—could suppress the entrepreneurial spirit of

Levy's Management Philosophy and Leadership Principles

"You can be really smart, but if you lose your integrity, you have nothing left."

1. *Trust*—Relationship building, candor, and integrity.

2. *Communication*—Educate, inform, and listen.

3. *Coach*—Mentor, support, challenge.

4. *Respect*—Treat everyone with respect and dignity.

5. *Visibility*—Walk around; you learn a lot.

6. *Timing*—Know when the time is right to move.

7. *Bias for Action*—No decision is a decision.

8. *Team Building*—Create a sense of purpose and commitment.

9. *Role Model*—What you say means a lot; what you do means even more.

10. *Caring and Giving*—We are in a people business and are here to serve those in need.

the individual company leaders. On the other hand, empowering them too much would undermine the moves toward more coordinated behavior and goals.

Stakeholders were essentially telling him as the top leader in the organization, "Give us the best of both possible worlds," or in other words, make sure the key players take risks the way they did before the restructuring *and* play it safe by leveraging the advantages of the new structure. It's an intricate change-leadership challenge for a CEO that is currently underway. Woodring's success to date in his leadership role has not only earned him respect within the company—the arrows are turning in the same direction—but he has also been recognized by his industry. On June 16, 2013, the board of directors of the International Insurance Society (IIS) elected Woodring Chairman of the IIS board of directors.

Becoming a Leader at Any Level

Leaders at every level face certain chronic, perennial tensions as well as conflicting needs that are ongoing for a period of time—for example, throughout a project's lifecycle. When leaders "wing it" and deal with those tensions on a case-by-case basis, they are likely to undermine their effectiveness and frustrate the people who look to them for consistency. For example, if the head of a public relations department has to serve the publicity needs of multiple company divisions, the people in those divisions would expect her to have a system of evaluating requests that's balanced and fair. If that's not the case, and her efforts seem random and subjective, that behavior will erode the perception of her as a leader. Behind closed doors—or maybe even within earshot of her—people will say, "Get rid of her!"

Paradox thinking supports consistent behavior in a leader. It provides a framework for maintaining a balanced perspective on opportunities and challenges, for keeping both potential positive and negative outcomes in view. I have found key leadership paradoxes include:

- Conditional respect _and_ unconditional respect.
- Technology focus _and_ relationship focus.
- Candor _and_ diplomacy.
- Responsibility _and_ freedom.
- Confidence _and_ humility.
- Analysis _and_ encouragement.
- Control _and_ empowerment.
- Grounded _and_ visionary.
- Logic _and_ creativity.
- Individual _and_ work group.
- Planning _and_ implementation.

You could easily use other terms for many of these pairings; it's important you rely on words you feel best capture the concept. For example, "control *and* empowerment" might also be captured as "tight *and* loose" or "taking charge *and* inviting initiative."

Seemingly conflicting needs such as those in the list don't have much meaning until the tensions they describe surface in your own life. At first glance, maybe you think none of them apply. Consider the different kinds of challenges or struggles you have in a workday, though, and you might realize that one or two do relate to your life. For example, you may wonder why the budget for your new project seems unsound, and then when you think about it, you realize that you are the sole contributor—but there are three other people working on the project who could probably help with the numbers. You might just have an "individual *and* work group" paradox in play.

As your career develops, it's likely that more and more of these paradoxes will have relevance. As you add new dimensions to your competencies, you may find yourself stretching in ways that invite paradox. For example, you may have begun your career with self-perception that you're mainly a tactician, but as you've taken on more complicated responsibilities, you find yourself spending more time focusing on the big picture.

The following is a sample of what I call a competency grid. It's an at-a-glance presentation of leadership characteristics that are generally necessary in an organization to be successful over the long term. As you go through the descriptions, try to get a sense of what applies to you, where you seem to be headed, and what descriptions don't seem applicable to you at all. The more the descriptions seem to apply, the more likely you are to have paradoxes like those listed previously have daily relevance for you.

	Performance	Leadership/ Development	Innovation
I N D I V I D U A L C O N T R I B U T O R	*Achievement Driver:* • Uses hard work and drive to accomplish quality outcomes. • Establishes and achieves deadlines and milestones. • Takes initiative even when situations are not clear. • Sets challenging goals and accepts responsibility for achieving them. • Uses time efficiently to accomplish objectives. • Seeks advice from experts in order to improve performance.	*Work Leader:* • Builds and develops work practices and skills. • Acquires new knowledge and skills to build areas of expertise. • Leverages strengths to coach and teach others. • Is open-minded and interested in views and perspectives of others. • Tries new things. • Learns from mistakes.	*Creative Problem-Solver:* • Evaluates information to generate innovative solutions. • Clearly defines the nature of the problem. • Identifies when enough information has been gathered to solve a problem. • Looks at a problem from multiple perspectives. • Identifies alternative solutions/scenarios. • Selects most appropriate solution.

	Performance	Leadership/ Development	Innovation
L E A D E R / M A N A G E R	*Implementation Driver:* • Ensures efficient and effective execution. • Successfully completes entrepreneurial efforts. • Effectively and efficiently manages processes, projects, and systems. • Effectively manages resources. • Makes tough, pragmatic decisions when necessary. • Identifies and shares best practices.	*Team Leader:* • Builds strong, effective, high-performance teams. • Challenges others with clear goals and responsibilities that result in achievement and ownership. • Helps access resources and overcome roadblocks for the team. • Motivates people to take responsibility, make decisions, and act on their own. • Leverages diversity. • Facilitates the continuous growth and development of individuals and teams. • Coaches, encourages, and provides balanced performance feedback.	*Innovative Thinker:* • Develops original solutions that ensure long-term organizational success. • Clarifies complex data or situations. • Outlines implications of decisions at the organizational level. • Defines and structures an issue despite incomplete or ambiguous information. • Identifies and focuses on the most critical high impact issues required for the organization to be successful. • Takes calculated entrepreneurial risks.

	Performance	Leadership/ Development	Innovation
S E N I O R L E A D E R	*Operations Driver:* • Drives operational excellence throughout the organization. • Focuses the organization on efforts that add value for customers, employees, and shareholders. • Executes both short- and long-term objectives. • Transforms strategy into results. • Regularly reviews business with leaders evaluating results against business plan. • Establishes processes for sharing best practices and managing knowledge.	*Organizational Leader:* • Builds organizational capability through people and processes. • Inspires others to perform their best. • Identifies and develops organizational capabilities necessary to achieve future business goals. • Facilitates continuous growth and development of individuals to improve bench strength. • Finds qualified and talented candidates from diverse backgrounds and experiences. • Aligns company values and capabilities to the business strategy to build and/or sustain corporate culture. • Establishes roles, responsibilities, reporting relationships that reflect and reinforce the corporate culture.	*Strategic Visionary:* • Develops a strategic vision for the business. • Identifies problems and issues not obvious to others. • Draws on experience to apply relevant models and approaches readily. • Creates new reasoning or models that explain complex situations. • Anticipates and stays ahead of competitive moves and changes rules when necessary. • Manages well in ambiguous situations. • Makes decisions with a cross-functional, cross-division perspective. • Drives innovation through people and processes.

No matter where you are in your organization, if you have willing followers, you are a leader. I urge you to embed the concept in your thinking rather than associate it with a title. Some CEOs are not leaders other than by position. They founded companies on the basis of an invention, inherited a position of senior authority, or perhaps had credentials that a board of directors saw as critical at the moment. None of these factors automatically makes someone a leader. Change leaders are all around us.

PART II

Implementing the Process

Chapter 5

Building the Model

> "Do not be misled by what you see
> around you, or be influenced by what
> you see. You live in a world which is
> a playground of illusion, full of false
> paths, false values and false ideals. But
> you are not part of that world."
> —Sai Baba, Indian guru

John Forbes Nash, Jr., the Nobel Prize–winning mathematician portrayed by Russell Crowe in *A Beautiful Mind* (2001) is well known for his theory of equilibrium. He famously called economist Adam Smith wrong for asserting that the best result comes from everyone in a group doing what's best for himself. Nash believes that Smith saw only half the picture—the competitive side. That didn't make sense to Nash, who concluded in *A Beautiful Mind* that "the best for the group comes when everyone in the group does what's best for himself AND the group." Nash is a consummate paradox thinker.

The meaning of seeing only half the picture becomes clear when you look at Rubin's vase (aka Rubin face), created by Danish psychologist Edgar Rubin:

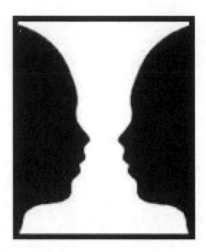

You can't see the faces unless the vase is present, and you can't see the vase unless the faces are present. They are the kind of interdependent pair that Nash described. All interdependent pairs, therefore all paradoxes, are inextricably linked.

Envision the Aim, the Miss, and Positive and Negative Outcomes

The interdependent sets are more than just linked. They represent the flow of energy. As you look at Rubin's reversing, two-dimensional image, you can only maintain one image at a time, even though you know they are both there. Once you've seen both elements of the picture, you are likely to switch back and forth between the vase and the faces. You can feel the energetic relationship between the images.

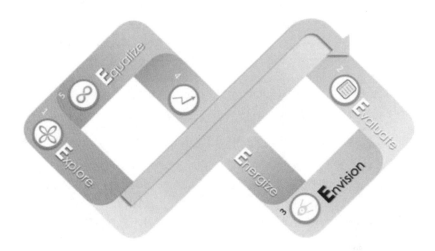

To depict this relationship between pairs in a paradox, I begin with an infinity loop—something that may once again remind of you John Nash if you saw *A Beautiful Mind*. The movie contains a memorable scene in which Nash (played by Russell Crowe) rides his bicycle in an infinity sign, which slowly solidifies into part of a mathematical formula from the next scene.[1]

The images that follow take the infinity loop visual further. They are the central part of a working model that helps us bring the concept of paradox into a practical tool to discover radically innovative solutions. Later, I engage you in an exercise where you build your own model.

Interdependent opposites are positioned in relation to one another within the loop. In the following example, they are stability and change:

- ◗ The arrows in the loop emphasize that the paradox represents an energy system.
- ◗ The fact that the loop is tight signifies, at this point, that you haven't begun the process of managing them; they co-exist in a state of interdependence—that's all.

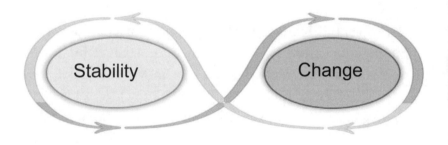

- ◗ When you over-focus on one part of the pair at the neglect of the other, you get the downside of it. So if you over-focus on stability, you get the negative effect of actions that support stability. The natural tendency is to then focus on change. But an over-focus on change brings you negative effects as well. This image depicts the negative effect of an over-focus on change:

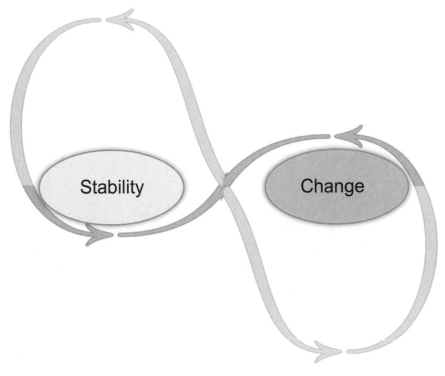

This image depicts success in managing both stability and change well because the loops push upward:

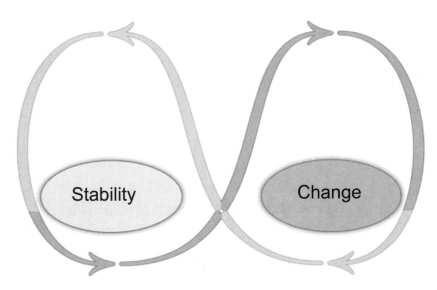

The next element of the model is adding the Aim at the top and the Miss at the bottom:

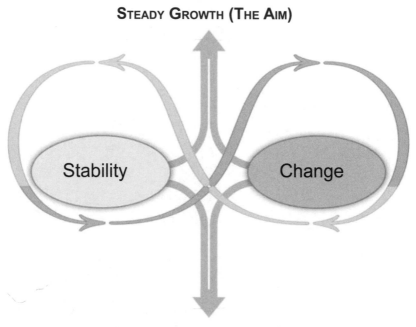

STEADY GROWTH (THE AIM)

Stability   Change

STEADY DECLINE (THE MISS)

The next is inserting the positive outcomes of focusing on each of the pairs, and the negative outcomes of over-focusing on one part of the pair at the neglect of the other. To illustrate how these positive and negative outcomes are plugged in, I'll use a few examples, the first of which is St. Louis Finance, introduced in Chapter 1.

The three paradoxes emerging from the six conflicting needs are:

1. Growth through financial advisors *and* growth through direct contact with customers.

2. Emphasis on people (talent) *and* emphasis on process.

3. Gathering data to understand customers *and* sharing data to demonstrate success.

In working with the St. Louis Finance marketing executive team, we developed a model for each pair of conflicting needs. We used the vocabulary of people on the team so the description of the positive and negative outcomes would ring true for them. That's very important in your own development of a model. **Rely on the language that is familiar** to you and/or your group, rather than pull catch phrases or academic jargon out of the latest trade publication article. The following model reflects the initial discussion of what successful and unsuccessful management of one, key pair would mean:

CLIENT GROWTH

- Speed to increased market share.
- Spreads risk.
- Skills already developed.

- Customer loyalty to company.
- Consistency of culture.
- Leadership control over business.
- Cheaper than acquisition.

Growth Through Acquisition of FAs — and — Growth Through Organic Means

- High cost of acquisition.
- High cost of turnover.
- Conflict between Co. and FA objectives.
- Challlenging decision making.

- Slow growth of market share.
- Time it takes to develop skills.
- Company bears the entire risk.

SLOW DECLINE OF BUSINESS

The next example spotlights a client organization my colleague Bill McKendree worked with. We discussed the issues facing this company, a real company cloaked here as SoCA Real Estate, after he had been advising them for a couple of months. Even if you have been going a traditional route in your meetings, you can bring the concept and models of paradox thinking into it and move forward with paradox thinking from that point on.

SoCA is widely known for its inventive approach to regional shopping malls. The company creates "destinations" by adding activities, art, inventive architecture and landscaping, and even a hotel to some of its retail developments. So is SoCA a business that builds and leases functional spaces—its original focus—or a company that lures tourists and groups looking for a unique conference location?

In identifying the Aims related to SoCA's business paradoxes, it's important to answer the question of what the company's core business is. But is it possible that it can be answered by a paradox? That is, can SoCA be legitimately described as both a regional mall developer and a resort/hospitality company? The Aim for SoCA does not suggest either one: sustainability over time. The main paradox that must be managed to achieve that Aim is client growth. If it's not managed well the Miss is that the company would have a slow decline in business.

Seeing what's involved with managing both sides of the paradox well, as well as what the downside looks like, gives insights as to how the company's CEO might be able to achieve a balancing act.

The positive outcomes of investing in growth include:

- Creates expanded market appeal.
- Builds new capacity.
- Gives new options around the core business.
- Provides new revenue streams.

The negative outcomes of investing in growth at the neglect of driving down expense mean the company:

- Runs out of capital.
- Undermines the current business by ignoring the original cash cow business.
- Accelerates a loss of market share of the core business.

The positive outcomes of driving down expense include:
- Capital to invest in growth and seek new opportunities.
- Making the operation generally more efficient.

The negative outcomes of driving down expense at the neglect of investment in growth leads to:
- Taking eyes off opportunities for the business.
- A lowered ability to respond to new opportunities.

Considering the negative outcomes that can result from over-focusing on one part of the pair at the neglect of the other, it's important to note the Miss—and to put it into the developing model:

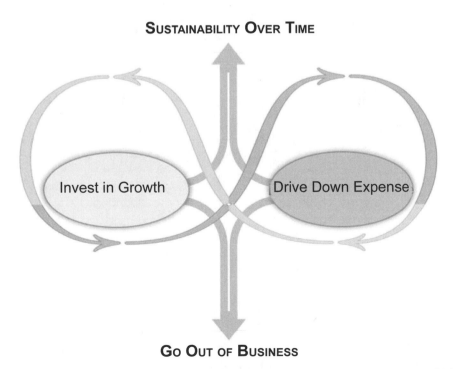

SUSTAINABILITY OVER TIME

Invest in Growth   Drive Down Expense

GO OUT OF BUSINESS

Filling in the model with those points gives a picture of the balancing act faced by the organization. The CEO may have these thoughts in mind, but the visual representation of them organizes them in a way that makes it easy to share and further explore with others in the company. At this stage, ideas are being generated as a result of brainstorming. Any model created at this point would be considered a draft, yet to be finalized.

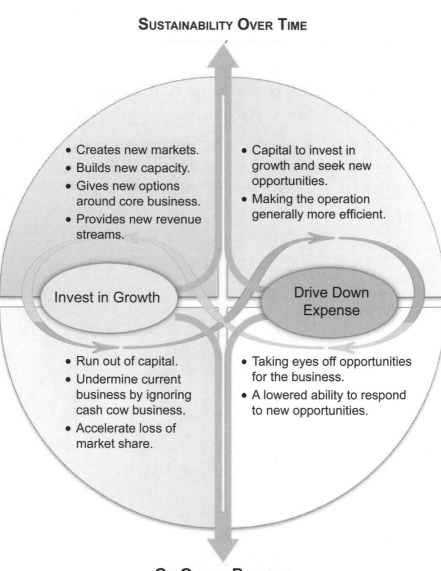

SUSTAINABILITY OVER TIME

- Creates new markets.
- Builds new capacity.
- Gives new options around core business.
- Provides new revenue streams.

- Capital to invest in growth and seek new opportunities.
- Making the operation generally more efficient.

Invest in Growth

Drive Down Expense

- Run out of capital.
- Undermine current business by ignoring cash cow business.
- Accelerate loss of market share.

- Taking eyes off opportunities for the business.
- A lowered ability to respond to new opportunities.

GO OUT OF BUSINESS

The next part of the process is cross-checking the positive and negative outcomes to see if they are expressed in a way that truly represents the tensions present in the paradox. Although there isn't a one-to-one correspondence in this draft SoCA model, there is a strong connection between the positive outcomes in the upper left quadrant and the negative outcomes in the lower right. There is a similar diagonal relationship between the positive outcomes listed for "drive down expense"

SUSTAINABILITY OVER TIME

- Outcomes all related to "new" markets, capacity, options around core business and revenue.

- Outcomes all related to "improved" cash position, efficiency.

Invest in Growth

Drive Down Expense

- Outcomes result from over-focus on growth; negatives are the price of trying too hard to get the "new."

- Outcomes result from over-focus on driving down expenses; negatives are the result of "starving" the business.

GO OUT OF BUSINESS

and the negative outcomes in the lower left quadrant. A summary of the relationships could be represented as shown on page 133.

When the teams came together at ITHRes, which was introduced in Chapter 1, their modeling of the positive and negative outcomes of the stability and change paradox yielded some surprising results. First, they decided to recast "stability and change" as "growth through core strength and growth through new strength." The former captures the sales and marketing team's idea that partnering with a company specializing in corporate moves from one facility to another would expand opportunities to supply the market with IT-skilled temporary help. The latter describes the technical team's vision of expanding their services into consulting and training.

Each team offered three positive and three negative outcomes:

In this instance the image shown on page 135, the diagonal relationships between the upsides and downsides came naturally. The teams just happened to take the approach that, if there was something positive that could come out of the action they proposed, then a counterpart negative outcome was a possibility as well. "Expand high-margin services" would be an expensive undertaking at first, so the negative they listed was "high cost of launching new services." "Make the brand more robust" certainly carried enormous potential for the company, but if the efforts resulted in "brand dilution," then the company would suffer greatly. And even though the thought of trying to "exploit and develop more skills of IT talent" engaged the technical team, the fact was that a drive to do so could result in "talent overwhelmed" and the technical team spreading themselves too thin.

The two teams came to a stark realization when they looked at possible outcomes: The cost of failing in the pursuit of "growth through new strength" was enormous—much larger than the negative outcomes of mismanaging the partnering option. An over-focus on growth through new strength could mean catastrophic losses of capital,

ACCELERATED GROWTH

- Leverage partners' network.
- Leverage partners' resources.
- Leverage partners' talent.

- Expand high-margin services.
- Make brand more robust.
- Exploit and develop skills of IT talent.

Growth Through Core Strength

Growth Through New Strength

- Over-reliance on partner network; complacency.
- Dependence on partners' stability.
- Reduced standards in vetting IT talent.

- High cost of launching new services.
- Brand dilution.
- Talent overwhelmed; spreading ourselves too thin.

TRAUMATIC DECLINE

erosion of brand identity, and an inability to meet needs with sufficient high-quality talent. In contrast, an over-focus on growth through core strength would result in a decline for the business, but it would be a decline from which recovery would take months, rather than put the entire company at risk.

Suddenly, instead of being at odds with one another, they realized that the technical team had a great idea, but the company couldn't afford it at the moment. Both teams then took a harder look at partnering and came up with a new paradox: growth through current model *and* growth through partnering model.

ACCELERATED GROWTH

- Reinforce current client relationships.
- Reinforce brand.
- Maintain high performance standards.

- Leverage partners' network.
- Leverage partners' resources.
- Leverage partners' talent.

Growth Through Current Model

Growth Through Partnering Model

- Miss out on new opportunities.
- Let brand get stale.
- Get complacent about performance; cease to innovate.

- Over-reliance on partner network; complacency.
- Dependence on partners' stability.
- Reduced standards in vetting IT talent.

TRAUMATIC DECLINE

In a significant way, ITHRes faced an interdependent set of opportunities that was very much like that of St. Louis Finance. It was a matter of fostering partner relationships that hopefully cascaded into many new clients *and* the cultivation of direct client relationships.

Exercise: Building Your Own Model

Building a useful visual that captures the upsides and downsides of both parts of your paradox is an energizing group activity, although you can also use the visual to organize your thoughts and to present them to your colleagues. What follows is a practical exercise you can use with your team; the steps are numbered to clarify that they build on those in the Chapter 3 exercise:

4.   Draw an infinity loop on a white board or a flip chart.
5.   Write the conflicting needs in the infinity loop, one on the left, one on the right.
6.   Brainstorm the positive and negative outcomes for each competing need. Note: Negative outcomes surface as a result of over-focus on one need at the neglect of the other.

This is an exercise that will continue to build over the next few chapters.

Long-Term Implications

At this point in the process, some companies take what they've learned and start building vision statements and planning documents that reflect the thinking they've done about managing pivotal paradoxes. This sample language from a museum strategic plan shows how a narrative can pull together the ideas of paradox, the Aim, the upsides, and the downsides.

The museum's Aim is to be "the premier art museum" for a certain type of collection. It will achieve that through developing "the strongest possible art and archival collections" and "forging alliances with other museums," which could be captured in the paradox "stand alone *and* partner with others," or simply "self *and* others."

In its discussion of what happens if the museum is successful in these efforts, the following positive outcomes are stated: "[the museum] attracts collectors, scholars, museum professionals, artists;" it also receives "major gifts" and "garners awards for excellence in best practices."

Take a look at the existing strategic plan for your organization and analyze it with the concepts of paradox, the Aim, and outcomes in mind. It's possible that you will arrive at the conclusion that your planning team subliminally (or consciously) grasped the concept of interdependent opposites and the plan reflects that understanding. It's also possible that, once you are wearing the lens that allows you to see paradox, your organization's plan may seem to have gaps or statements that don't support each other. In the next planning cycle, that will all be different!

Chapter 6

Developing Action Steps

"Actions are always more complex and
nuanced than they seem. We have to
be willing to wrestle with paradox in
pursuing understanding."
—Sir Harold Evans, journalist

Evaluating the paradoxes that apply to your business helps remind
you of the context in which your organization operates. Exploring those
paradoxes by looking at the positive outcomes of managing them well
and the negative outcomes of over-focusing on just one part should
increase your situational awareness. In this next phase, you arrive at the
point where you need to know your context even more deeply: Based
on your knowledge of your business environment and the opportunities
and challenges that lie therein, you will now determine the action steps
that will get you where you want to go.

Energize the Solution

How will you gain or maintain the positive results from focusing
on each part of the pair? Who will take the actions, and when will they
take them? As you start to answer these questions, begin brainstorming. Avoid constraining thoughts and focus on surfacing the actions.

Don't worry how big or small an action might be; a seemingly small action might be a key driver for other actions. Later in the process, you will go back and clean up and rethink what the final actions need to be; you will want to restate many of them when you plot them as action steps in your model, or even as objectives in the action plan.

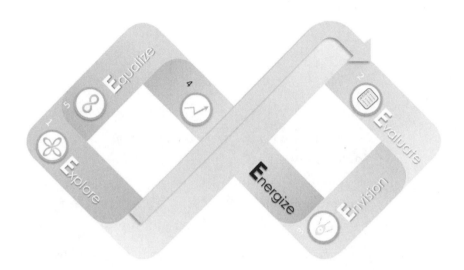

Exercise: Plotting Actions on the Model

These steps build on the exercise begun in Chapter 3 and continued in Chapter 5. Here, a combination of either/or and both/and thinking will serve you well.

7. Focusing on the left side of your model, determine the actions that are necessary to achieve the stated positive outcomes

8. Focusing on the right side of your model, determine the actions that are necessary to achieve the stated positive outcomes

9. Once actions have been generated, reflect on the following questions.

When creating action steps as part of a group planning effort, it's highly likely that the question "what action steps should we take to get these positive outcomes?" will yield some strong opinions—some based on experience, some on research, some on intuition.

When someone offers an idea—or if you are going through this process solo—to get the combination of either/or and both/and approaches going, ask some questions:

▶ How does the proposed action step correlate to a specified need? **Example:** The paradox might be "measure customer satisfaction *and* take immediate action to improve customer satisfaction." A proposed action of "interact with customers" might need to be split into two and used as an action step for both needs—that is, "interact with customers to get their feedback on our service *and* interact with customers to improve customer service in real time."

▶ Is there more than one way to do that? **Example:** The action proposed is for the CEO to focus more heavily on joint ventures. Because there isn't anyone as qualified to analyze and act on joint ventures, there is no alternative. **Example:** A proposed action to "staff up" in a particular business area might be addressed by adding contractors if the need may not be ongoing.

▶ Does the action reflect what we know about the business environment? **Example:** The action proposed to expand the law firm is to hire more attorneys who have experience in real estate. If real estate transactions are trending downward, that may not be a wise move.

   ▶ Within the question, therefore, is a corollary: What do you know about the business environment that would accelerate positive results from the action and what do you know that would inhibit positive results?

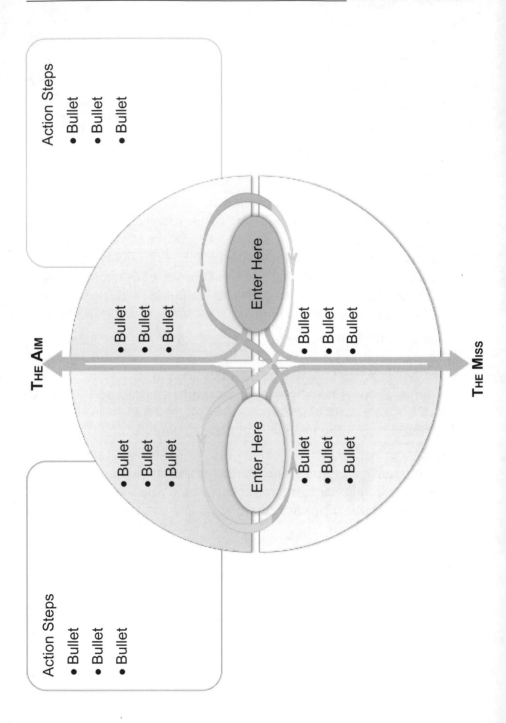

Real Actions, Real Outcomes

The actions of Affirm Health show that the organization's leaders were tuned into managing conflicting needs and they drew on some tried-and-true programs, as well as innovative practices, to support that effort.

The company's CEO supported the creation of a book for all employees specifying a goal of clinically excellent care with no preventable injuries or deaths and said this would be achieved through:

- Work on a culture of safety.
- Commitment to learning from one another, sharing successes and disseminating best practices.
- Commitment to work together toward care that is safe, effective, patient-centered, timely, efficient, and equitable.

Complementary to this effort, he set in place an ambitious 10-year plan begun in 2008 that encompasses a goal of absolute patient satisfaction. Woven into these plans were upgrades to facilities as well and, as noted in Chapter 1, Affirm created the position of senior vice president, facilities task force.

Affirm therefore is managing the pivotal paradox of "clinical needs *and* facilities needs" as well as the pairs nested inside of clinical needs and facilities needs, including one nested inside of clinical needs we'll call "measuring patient satisfaction *and* taking action on patient satisfaction."

To reiterate briefly the issues related to "clinical needs *and* facilities needs" that were covered in Chapter 1 and Chapter 2, a solitary focus on the requirements for providing superior care means that elevators might break down. In contrast, making facilities needs the priority means resources available to purchase and install medical equipment might be diverted to fix the elevator.

One representation of various pairs of needs that would all live inside of "clinical needs"is shown here.

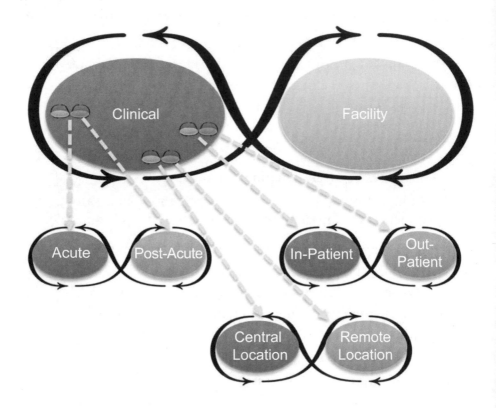

The paradox related to patient satisfaction—that is, "measuring patient satisfaction *and* taking action on patient satisfaction"—would be nested inside both "in-patient" and "out-patient."

Actions that would help Affirm create the positive outcomes they want in both the clinical and facilities area include those listed on the following model shown on page 145.

Drilling down into clinical needs, the issue of patient satisfaction has an interdependent pair: measuring patient satisfaction *and* taking action on patient satisfaction. On the "measuring" side, the company

SERVICE EXCELLENCE

SERVICE FAILURES

Facilities Needs

Clinical Needs

- Efficient reliable physical plant.
- State-of-the-art equipment.
- Positive environment for patients and providers.

- Culture of safety.
- Shared best practices.
- Patient satisfaction.

- More concern for things than people.
- Physical plants not in support of best practices.
- Erosion of patient-centered approach.

- Degradation of physical plant.
- Insufficient investment in equipment upgrades.
- Facilities-related challenges to providing patient care.

Action Steps
- Create plan that aligns strategies for facilities with clinical mission/goals.
- Improve clinical efficiencies.
- Measure facilities impact on quality of healthcare.
- Assess staff productivity relative to facilities.

Action Steps
- Reinforce elements of culture that drive patient safety.
- Clarify the business case for clinical excellence.
- Invest in infrastructure to support innovation and quality care.
- Standardize best practices and share them with the team.

145

could use something like Net Promoter to guide actions related to defining the patient experience, involvement of senior management, and then ultimately applying the customer loyalty metric—Net Promoter Score—developed by Fred Reichheld, Fain & Company, and Satmetrix. NPS scores range from –100 (everyone is a detractor) to +100 (everyone is a promoter).[1] Earning a score of +50 or above is considered excellent. The way that Affirm could handle the process of preparing to implement Net Promoter could embed actions related to improving patient satisfaction at the same time they were measuring it.

The *Harvard Business Review* article "Winning Results with NPS" suggests how a company like Affirm could move step-by-step toward implementing Net Promoter:

- Set up an NPS team at the corporate level.
- Compile research related to patient experiences and establish a common language to discuss patient experiences.
- Have the team begin communicating with the CEOs of the individual hospitals about their work and findings.
- Send out regular information on NPS, including a report highlighting where each local system and each individual hospital stood relative to others.
- Have members of the NPS team regularly visit hospitals and use a systematic approach to studying patients' experiences. That would give them an opportunity to talk with middle managers and frontline employees about NPS and how to foster loyalty.

When plotted on a model, the action steps related to managing both parts of the pair can be represented like this:

ABSOLUTE PATIENT SATISFACTION

PATIENT MISERY

Action Steps
- Conduct research and define patient experience.
- CEOs share research across the system of hospitals.
- Develop integrated organization-wide scorecard reporting protocol.
- Utilize Net Promoter System.

Action Steps
- Identify factors that matter most to patients.
- Identify best practices and trouble spots with real-time feedback.
- Empower staff to put patient needs first, raise productivity, eliminate waste.
- Align people practices.

Measuring Patient Satisfaction
- Discover desired patient experience.
- Define patient satisfaction.
- Determine effectiveness of delivering on the desired experience.

- Patients complain about lack of responsiveness to their needs.
- Overabundance of questions.
- Multitudes of studies.

Taking Action on Patient Satisfaction
- Priority attention given to patient satisfaction.
- Issues surfaced and addressed.
- Targeted improvements made that directly and positively impact the patient experience.

- Miss systemic shifts in needs if too narrowly focused.
- Organization overwhelmed with activity
- Overlook out-patient needs.

The research and information gathering related to the Net Promoter metric can allow the organization to map out a plan of action that related directly to patient satisfaction and safety.

Actions That Trigger Success—and Failure

A single action or decision generally does not lead to the bankruptcy or decline of a company, although it is possible for that to happen. In this section, I spotlight the paradox or set of paradoxes that a company faced before it failed financially, and how a choice to go with an either/or approach led to that outcome. I also want to stimulate your thinking about what would managing the paradox have looked like, and to plot out how a different course would either have averted the bankruptcy or decline completely, or mitigated the downward plunge. Another objective of this section is pointing out companies that sat at the top of the glacier, poised to slide down it uncontrollably, and instead, they hiked to territory where they could maintain their footing.

Some of the companies discussed in this section are the embodiment of paradox: They are successes and failures at the same time. Whether the company would be viewed as one rather than the other depends purely on the definition of the Aim. When executives, shareholders, creditors, employees, and customers have different and conflicting perceptions of what constitutes the Aim for the organization in a given circumstance, then it's highly likely that one group's success is another group's failure.

Hostess Brands is a perfect example of that paradox of success and failure. If Hostess executives had cared as much about the company's workers as consumers cared about the products those workers produced, we may not have had the Great Twinkies Crisis of 2012. At the same time, if worker engagement and baking great snacks were corporate priorities, then those executives would not have been positioned to rake in $860+ million by selling off pieces of a company that had an estimated worth of only $450 million.

Paradoxes of leadership and organization faced by the company in the years leading up to bankruptcy included those of an established organization, as described in Chapter 3. Among them were:

- Self (leaders focused on self) *and* others (leaders focused on organization).

- Delivering on current customer needs *and* awareness of changing needs signaled in the market.

- Taking the time for making improvements and changes *and* increasing efficiency/productivity and speed in responding to customer needs.

- Mission *and* margin.

It's always important to look at the environment and context a company operates in, as well as key issues that come up for them and never seem to go away—chronic struggles—in order to understand how applicable these classic paradoxes are to the company. Here are just a few factors for Hostess that relate to the conflicting needs previously expressed:

- Hostess had six CEOs in the ten year period prior to the bankruptcy of 2012.

- The company faced intractable union negotiators on workplace-reform issues and finally broke its union contracts by not paying pension benefits. One of the key unions undermined attempts to increase efficiency by enforcing work rules that slowed down product distribution. That is, they slowed down the process of meeting customer needs.

- Wages and benefits to workers were cut at the same time salaries for senior executives rose.

- The senior financial team was populated with extremely high-paid consultants rather than in-house talent.

- The company produced the same high-fat, high-sugar, low-fiber products it has made for years in an environment where the appeal of healthy and/or low-carbohydrate foods has been trending upward. In this same business environment, Coca Cola and General Mills made adjustments to product offerings and have thrived.

▶ The company's response to growing demand for lower-calorie products was to introduce Twinkie Bites, which are simply smaller versions of Twinkies.

▶ Hostess management never made the investment in new machinery and new technology that executives promised in getting a $110 million concession from the bakery union after the company's 2004 bankruptcy. Over the years, the union asserted that this hurt the company.

Mainstream media coverage of the Hostess debacle suggested that two main factors combined to take the company down: decisions reflecting mismanagement and union demands culminating in a strike. Even without delving more deeply into the hedge-fund and union problems of Hostess as the trade press and industry analysts did, this pair of actions would find their place on a model built around the paradox "self *and* others."

The positive side of managing "self" would include assertive leadership and tight scheduling of time. The positive side of managing "others" would include thoughtful decision-making and accessibility to employees.

Over-focusing on "self"results in uncaring decision-making and lack of accessibility to employees. Similarly, over-focusing on "others" leads to leadership and an extreme open-door policy.

Let's step back from this set of ups and downs and consider what type of actions that executives would take if focused on "self":

▶ Shoring up executive compensation packages.

▶ Hiring consultants to reinforce the position of executives.

▶ Legal protection in the event of corporate failure.

▶ Hard bargaining with the unions regarding their demands.

The type of actions they would take if focused on "others" would be:

▶ Recruiting and retaining top talent so that the organization's bench strength at the senior levels would ensure sound management.

▶ Responding to worker warnings that certain manufacturing equipment was outdated.

▶ Communicating with workers about the gravity of carrying significant debt.

The Aim for the paradox of "self *and* others" could be built on the corporate slogan "Serving up family time one smile at a time." The Miss could be "Failing to make the customers smile."

From a different point of view, however, the Aim might be expressed as "Making the most money with the least number of people." And the Miss might be "Losing money due to a bloated workforce."

Because the company seemed to operate out of balance for so many years—the 2012 bankruptcy was its second in less than a decade—I would be inclined to call Hostess a failure. But consider that there are those who would assert the executive team of company scored a big success. They got out of the baking business, which required a large workforce, and made a lot of money (which the creditors appreciated) by stripping down to a liquidation team of about 200 executives who sold off pieces of a company for twice what the company was worth. The price of success was 18,000 jobs.

In introducing this section on failed companies, I mentioned that you might want to plot out how a different course would either have averted the bankruptcy completely or mitigated the downward plunge. It is a highly useful exercise that you can do on two levels: You can do it based solely on the data provided in this book, or you can use that information as a starting point and delve deeply into the facts of the case through additional research.

Schwinn Bicycles failed 11 years before Hostess, but it was out of balance in some strikingly similar ways. Schwinn had legacy products and a brand with household familiarity. To many consumers who grew up in the 1960s, "Schwinn" meant "bike." That is, it became generic-ized to some extent, just as Kleenex referred to any facial tissue. The early 1960s were a peak time for Schwinn, a company founded in 1895, partly because of high tariff rates on foreign-made bikes that remained in place until 1964.

Shortly afterward Schwinn's chronic struggles related to consumer demand and manufacturing methods took shape. They had the opportunity to manage two classic paradoxes of established companies:

1. Delivering on current customer needs _and_ awareness of changing needs signaled in the market.
2. Taking the time for making improvements and changes _and_ increasing efficiency/productivity and speed in responding to customer needs.

Regarding the first paradox, not once, but three times, the company's leadership failed to see the importance of changes in their current environment so they could not see the future. The first occasion was the onset of the 10-speed craze of the early 1970s. Right about the same time, BMX bikes became popular—and stayed popular, taking center stage at some of the most exciting winter and summer extreme-sports events. (What were retired Schwinn executives thinking in 2008 when BMX racing, the sport they criticized as being so dangerous that wouldn't make bikes for it, became an Olympic event?) The third failure later in that decade came when they dismissed mountain bikes as another ridiculous California fad.

Regarding the second paradox, by the time Schwinn executives realized they were missing the key trends in bicycles, their factory was too out-of-date to compete against those who had caught the trends. They didn't have the materials or the equipment to go head-to-head with European, Asian, and other U.S. manufacturers who dominated in the world of 10-speeds, BMX, and mountain bikes.

This is hard-driving either/or behavior that sends a company downhill without brakes. Typical responses to the eventual realization that customer needs have changed are catch-up tactics with a sharp focus on short-term gain:

- Outsource parts production.
- Turn from manufacturing to assembly, and as a corollary, do the assembly work where there is cheap labor.

For Schwinn, those tactics failed as well because their competition in Asia could still manufacture better bikes at lower cost than they could; they didn't have to outsource anything and could do the entire process with the cheapest labor. So, Schwinn headed further down the road they put themselves on in making the initial either/or decisions:

- Outsource production, thereby becoming a marketer, not a manufacturer.

Despite the succession of failures, the Schwinn name retained some value and Questor Partners Fund, which bought it in 1997, recognized that. What they did reflected an innate sense of paradox in envisioning Schwinn as old company *and* new company.

They purchased GT Bicycles, which had a reputation for innovation in mountain bikes, and paired their expertise with the Schwinn name. But it was too late. The Schwinn name just did not have credibility with the new generations of sport bikers. Schwinn was dad's bike. In her 2000 book, *Lessons From the Edge*, published the year before Schwinn/ GT declared bankruptcy, author Maryann Karinch interviewed Aaron Bethlenfalvy, the award-winning senior industrial designer for GT, and shared photos of the work the company was doing for top racers. The name "Schwinn" never entered the conversation, nor was it mentioned in the book. Bethlenfalvy is still a top designer and GT continues its life and good reputation under new ownership.

In this next example, I look at an industry success story and how the behavior of that organization contrasts with multiple companies in the same industry that went into sharp decline after the recession of 2008.

Theoretically, we need lawyers in good times and bad, but particularly in bad times. That is why even some industry analysts expressed surprised at the extent to which some prominent and large law firms downsized beginning in 2008. A few even chose to dissolve. In October 2008 alone, the Bureau of Labor Statistics reported that the legal services industry lost more than 1,000 jobs.[2] As of December 11, 2011, at least 15,435 people had been laid off by major law firms (5,872 lawyers and 9,563 staff) since January 1, 2008.[3] Some of the characteristics of firms that suffered include:

- Adherence to traditional, hourly billing practices.
- Business weighted toward areas where activity sharply decreased such as corporate litigation and real estate.
- Focus on partners' ability to finance the firm's operations through new deals.

There will likely always be market forces that catch organizations off guard. It's reasonable to expect that a law firm specializing in corporate litigation or real estate would meet tough times if cases in those areas start to dry up. They recruited talent that suddenly wasn't needed to the extent that it had been. At the same time, the other two factors, if approached with a paradox mentality, could substantially help a firm face a shifting and troublesome economic climate.

For example, in the wake of the recession, the research firm Acritas stated that 32 percent of the 600 executives they interviewed expected law firm billing practices to change in the near future. What Acritas heard was that companies intended to push firms toward billing flat fees, fixed fees, or success fees, which reflect a premium for an agreed-upon win. That evidence suggests that a firm would be wise to manage the paradox: hourly rates *and* alternative billing practices.

Focusing on partners as rainmakers *and* team players is another paradox coming out this analysis. With an eye on growth rather than downsizing, a mid-sized New England law firm recognized the value of the paradox and sought to manage it. The firm, a client of my colleague Wendy Helmkamp, employs more than 100 attorneys and is located in six U.S. cities.

For the firm, the paradox is nested within culture and inferred as individualistic *and* collaborative. Their growth strategy requires that they be entrepreneurial, yet they also need to be more collaborative in order to realize cross-selling opportunities and to expand client relationships for greater penetration and retention. The Aim giving it meaning is "growth over time" with the Miss being "going into decline." The latter is another way of expressing the outcome of becoming a mature company rather than remaining an established one. Another paradox related to the Aim is short-term financial gain *and* long-term viability.

A focus on the positive side of the entrepreneurial part of the pair yields good quarterly numbers and line-of- sight precision in exploiting opportunities. But too much focus on individual pursuits at the neglect of a collaborative culture means emphasis on key partners only (translation: rainmakers) and an individual-based approach to growth. This is precisely the kind of weighting that contributed to the dazzling rise and shocking decline of some competing firms. The lesson in this is that if your organization has a pendulum swing with a dramatic flair in the direction of profits, you might want to think in terms of physics and the effect of "restoring forces" (in this case, market forces) that will pull it toward the negative.

The firm's leadership stepped back to look at what circumstances might suggest that kind of over-emphasis on an individualistic culture. One was that the different offices of the firm were not interacting. Another was that more senior lawyers were not always bringing more junior lawyers into the relationship with key clients, putting at risk longer-term sustainability. It was as though they were taking a very narrow view of a key goal and stated aim of the firm that starts with the words: "Client service begins with interdisciplinary teams of regulatory, litigation and transactional attorneys...."

A focus on the positive side of the collaborative culture part of the pair means broadened capabilities, client retention, all partners thinking cohesively about growth, cross-team successes, and mentoring of partners in business development. Over-focus on that side at neglect of short-term individual gains could mean some attorney defections that could impact near term financial numbers.

The firm's approach invites its attorneys to look at the Rubin vase/face picture from earlier and embrace the reality that one doesn't exist without the other. As further proof of having a paradoxical mindset, the firm states openly that it will entertain alternative fees.

Similarly, Scottrade has been aggressive about staying at the forefront of trends in its arena. And as the company says on its Website, "As a result, Scottrade has experienced continued stability and steady growth." While Scottrade gained momentum, a number of financial services companies suffered severe declines or went out of business.

Among the many financial services companies that would make a list of business failures, these are the companies that hit bottom in 2008 and 2009:

- Allco Finance Group.
- Countrywide Financial.
- Lehman Brothers.
- Madoff Investment Securities.
- Wachovia.
- Washington Mutual.
- CIT Group.
- Colonial Bankgroup.

With some, it's obvious what the central either/or-related failure was. For example, Bernard Madoff chose an illegal business model as opposed to a legal one; Lehman Brothers chose to pursue astronomical profits over balanced, steady growth. With others, the decisions that doomed them involved more complexities. The important note is the contrast between the failed companies and a company like Scottrade.

While other financial services companies were closing their doors, Scottrade had almost explosive growth in the same period, going from 200 branch offices in 2004 to 500 by 2010. And during the height of the recession, Scottrade did not lay off any of its associates; in fact, the opposite occurred: They hired about 1,000 new associates and opened 75 new branches when so many other financial services companies were in crisis mode.

I met with senior executives, including the CEO, to get different perspectives on the challenges and opportunities the company faces. Combining their input, we arrived at more than a dozen paradoxical situations inside of what Scottrade is doing to effect change. Scottrade is a success story because the company is facing change head-on. That in itself makes the paradox of stability and change of central concern: In the midst of aggressive change, they know their ability to sustain customer loyalty is linked to the practices and skills that have made them great. They cannot afford to ignore the factors that helped the company maintain momentum in one of the most difficult periods faced by the financial services industry in modern times.

To close the discussion of either/or decisions and related actions that have put companies in a tailspin, a quick look at Send the Light (STL) illuminates a common mistake. A meteoric rise in profits, largely due to policies implemented by a savvy CEO, put the distributor of Christian books in a cash-rich position. The not-for-profit gobbled up a few other Christian booksellers, rising to become the 74th-largest charity in the United Kingdom in 2001. STL entered the American market a couple of years later and then merged International Bible Society to give it a global presence. The move meant the formation of one of the world's largest not-for-profit book distributors.

The pendulum had swung wildly the other way by 2009. On November 16, 2009, the company announced plans to sell operations due to financial challenges. They cited a succession of financial problems, but blamed one action more than others: "failed implementation of a new SAP computer system."[4]

A highly successful company that can point to a single action as the prime reason for its collapse is a company that has not managed paradoxes—at all. Their rise to success reflected decisions made by a leader based on his financial and marketing acumen. Actions that followed seemed to be taken in consideration of only one way of doing things: use the cash on hand to effect aggressive growth through acquisitions.

Represented as stacked paradoxes, the previous model is one way of looking at what happened to Send the Light. It also applies to so many other companies that perpetuated an uncompromising commitment to growth, change, and authoritarian decision-making at the expense of the company's stability and appreciation for talent at various levels of the organization. Very simply, they had no balance in their approach to opportunities or problem-solving.

Chapter 7

Identifying and Using Metrics to Stay on Target

A parable: *A man was examining the construction of a cathedral. He asked a stone mason what he was doing chipping the stones, and the mason replied, "I am making stones." He asked a stone carver what he was doing. "I am carving a gargoyle." And so it went. Each person said in detail what they were doing. Finally he came to an old woman who was sweeping the ground. She said, "I am helping build a cathedral."*

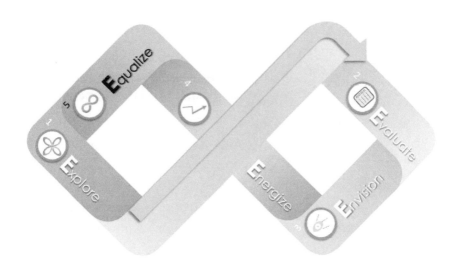

As in the above parable, most of the time each of us is immersed in the details of one special part of the whole and does not think of how what he is doing relates to the larger picture.

Action steps help you to achieve and manage positive outcomes. Metrics are a valuable tool in assessing risk; they indicate when you are starting to plunge into negative territory and need to adjust your action steps. Obsession with arbitrary metrics, however, can kill an organization, so it's important to identify measurements that have value in helping you achieve the Aim and avert the Miss.

Equalize the Execution

The term metrics suggests precision, numbers, and tables containing analytic data. Those certainly have a role in measurements of business, but there is also a softer side. In fact, the metrics related to many organizational challenges are paradoxes:

Quantitative _and_ qualitative.

Analytical _and_ intuitive.

Objective _and_ subjective.

Product/service _and_ process.

In this list, the metrics we might call "hard" are on the left, and those we might call "soft" are on the right. These sets have lots of overlap because there are multiple ways to express related concepts.

In the world of paradox, metrics are tied to both the results of actions taken, and to the positive and negative outcomes conceived in the planning stages. For example, a regional bank decided that both stability and change are desirable. Positive outcomes related to the positive aspects of change included competitive edge, increased customer satisfaction, and growth in assets. The bank closed one branch and concurrently enhanced online services. Results in the first quarter after the changes occurred were increased use of the Website for transactions, slightly longer lines at the remaining branches, and a seemingly flat level in the number of transactions overall. The metrics the bank executives needed to evaluate whether they were managing to the upside were both data-based and insight-based.

They needed data on the value of the transactions at the branches and online, what type of transactions were being made through both physical and Web-based services, how many transactions were completed at the remaining branches, what percentage increase those branch transactions represented of the overall business for the quarter, and the number of customers either lost or gained in the period. They also needed feedback from customers on the loss of the branch and the increase in Website services, a sense of what could be improved within the new operational model, and observations from people on the front lines of customer service—tellers, loan officers, and investment advisors—regarding how customers were responding to the new model.

| Metrics indicate risk to inform actions. | Actions drive outcomes. | Outcomes move you toward the Aim or the Miss. |

Regardless of whether the metrics are hard or soft, they are information only. Just because half the people who provide feedback on the Website think that a 12-character alpha-numeric password is a burdensome requirement doesn't mean that the bank should react by changing to an eight-character password. Perhaps that feedback and other metrics suggest that the bank did dip into negative territory during that quarter. **Taking action without looking at the balancing factors related to stability might only make it worse.**

Reinsurance Group of America (RGA) would appear to be all about the numbers: the value of portfolios, level of risk, yield on investments, and so on. Some key metrics for the company, however, are decidedly subjective.

As discussed in Chapter 1 and Chapter 4, RGA experienced major changes in 2008 and 2011 that had an impact on the role of CEO Greig Woodring. RGA began operating in the United States in 1973 as a reinsurance division of General American Life Insurance Company. Twenty years later, it became a holding company for General American's reinsurance operations. Throughout the 1990s, the company opened offices in several overseas locations and then was subsumed by Metropolitan Life Insurance when MetLife acquired RGA's mother company. In 2008, after expanding its global presence by bringing its total number of foreign offices to 20, RGA split off from MetLife. And then in 2011, it became a matrix organization and started to move toward more integrated systems instead of running like a loosely affiliated group of disconnected companies.

RGA is composed of reinsurance companies. Their client insurance companies seek reinsurance services to reduce their risk, but in this business, high risk often means high reward. Life insurance for a top racecar driver costs a lot more than it does for a healthy fifth-grade teacher of the same age; so, hypothetically, a company with a portfolio that includes insurance for several racecar drivers is higher risk as well as potentially higher reward. It is in the reinsurance company's interest to acquire those high-risk assets, keeping in mind that they need to be underwritten well and complemented by some safer assets.

A central paradox for the individual companies that make up RGA is my business *and* corporate perspective. Nested within "my business" is take risks *and* play it safe. "My business" refers to the entrepreneurial modus operandi and priorities that helped build RGA into one of the largest life reinsurance groups in the world. "Corporate perspective" is the headquarters, big-picture view of how to make the whole greater than the sum of its parts. The Aim is that the company, whole and parts, have a steadily improving bottom line; the Miss is that RGA goes out of business.

The positive outcomes of managing "my business" well include a number of factors, all under the general expectation that the businesses are doing exactly what is expected of them. Those upsides are:

- Performance expectations met.
- Revenues increasing.
- Profit streams increasing.
- Building value for their business.
- Control over their assets, which enables them to serve their client companies well.

Over-focusing on "my business" at the neglect of the "corporate perspective" results in downsides such as:

- Unleashing overly aggressive behavior in terms of the individual businesses bringing on risk.
- A distortion of business performance; those businesses that were not able to get more high-risk/high-yield assets into their portfolio would appear not to be performing well by comparison.
- Development of a power culture—that is, those in charge of the businesses with sizzling portfolios wield more power in the group.

Letting the parts be as entrepreneurial as they wished would work against the strength of the organization as a whole.

Focusing on the "corporate perspective" theoretically yields these positive outcomes:

◗ Optimizing the whole.

◗ Maintaining a big-picture perspective.

◗ Protection of the whole business.

◗ Creating value for the corporation.

◗ Having an overall safer method of operating for the corporation.

In contrast, over-focus on the "corporate perspective" at the neglect of "my business" would likely lead to:

◗ Lack of growth.

◗ Lack of innovation.

◗ Development of a centralized power culture.

◗ Complacency in the businesses, because the individual would be waiting for someone to take care of them instead of striking out to survive on his or her own.

Woodring said a lot about the corporate culture when the discussion of this last set of negatives caused him to remark, "I don't think we'd ever go that way. If anything, we'd swing too heavily in the direction of 'my business.'"[1] That kind of observation is key, not only in creating action steps, but also in evaluating outcomes. It supports the idea that metrics for success must be balanced between hard data that would pick winners and losers among the member businesses based on income stream, and more qualitative and subjective measures that consider soft factors like client satisfaction and adherence to corporate standards.

The one action step that Woodring knew he needed to take for the benefit of both sides of the paradox was to hire a senior person with asset liability responsibility. He knew it needed to be somebody who could deal with the enterprise holistically and keep focused on continually managing the tension between the individual businesses and the corporate entity. That's the person who would be most front-line in terms of using metrics to evaluate outcomes. On the quantitative side—relying on hard numbers—he would need tools to measure risk, liquidity, and protection, among other things. On the qualitative side, he would need consistent ways of collecting and filtering insights and opinions.

Woodring had another dimension of reflection—himself. He captured his own paradox in the words *self* and *the custodian of the statue*.

When focused on "self," positive outcomes include:

- Strengthened client relationships, resulting in increased revenue.
- Strong and consistent strategic guidance and planning for the organization.
- The ability to say, "I enjoy myself."

But when he over-focuses on "self," people around him often read the wrong meaning in what he says casually, and they tend to get edgy as an unintended consequence.

An emphasis on being "the custodian of the statue" brings positive outcomes such as:

- The company running well.
- People getting what they expect from him.
- Being more accessible to people in the company who need answers and guidance.

Over-focusing on "the custodian of the statue" at the neglect of "self" creates stress. His expressed concern was the he could end up feeling like a polisher of the statue—someone consumed by duty who is not taken seriously as a leader.

His personal Aim is that he is an effective CEO. His personal Miss is that he's an ineffective CEO. But he realizes that addressing his own paradox is also essential to achieving the Aim of bottom-line success for the company.

With a paradox like Woodring's, data-based metrics such as revenue increases on his watch indicate something about his ability to manage to the positive side of both. But looking at the keywords and key concepts in his positive statements gives a much richer sense of meaningful measurements of success: strong relationships, consistent guidance, personal enjoyment, a smooth-running company, the meeting of expectations, his availability as a resource.

The array of metrics that are valuable to RGA, therefore, is composed of hard and soft measurements of whether or not action steps are helping the company manage opposite needs. At the same time, Woodring has to fulfill leadership responsibilities so that the action steps are executed well and timed appropriately. To keep himself balanced, he also benefits from hard and soft metrics.

When Metrics Undermine Success

Research firms have a number of quantitative criteria they use to measure the performance of companies. Among them are:

- Most recent annual sales.
- One-year sales growth.
- Most recent year's net income.
- One-year net income growth.
- Total assets.
- Net profit margin.
- One-year employee growth.

Unfortunately, it's quite common for companies to build plans around achieving good numbers in these categories to the neglect of other business needs. At that point, the metrics don't serve an informational purpose; instead, they drive programs.

In terms of sales, over and over again we see that the desire to "hit the numbers" means a yearly or even semi-yearly revision of the compensation package for the sales force. Just as the sales team gets used to one set of incentives, they are replaced by another because someone in charge had a short-sighted, bright idea on how to "hit the numbers."

I know a trade association whose board of directors studied metrics related to association success and built the executive team's performance goals around them. A key goal for the president, who had already been an effective leader at the organization for 15 years, was to increase the number of members. The following year, the board evaluated the president's performance and concluded they should fire him because he had not increased membership. He explained that dues and fees were up because participation by the member companies in various programs had gone up. He also noted the organization's increased influence in the industry due to taking the lead in key lobbying efforts. His final statement, which he thought was quite compelling, was that not one member company had dropped out since he had taken over the presidency, and staff turnover was extremely low. Nonetheless, they replaced him with a man who charged in, ready to increase membership. He succeeded in doing so and the board felt self-satisfied that they had done the right thing. For the next three years, however, they saw overall revenue decline due to diminished participation in programs, increased staff turnover at the senior level, and expenses related to recruiting new members, such as inviting prospects to attend conferences for free.

What the board did is known in the vernacular as the tail wagging the dog. Ford Motor Company made a classic blunder by taking this approach—although in all fairness, Ford is neither alone in this tack nor should the company be characterized by what happened.

Prior to introducing the Pinto to the American market in 1971, Ford engineers alerted executives that the design made it a certainty that the car's gas tank would explode when struck from the rear. But the senior team was ruled by metrics: They would consider the venture a success if the car did not weigh more than 2,000 pounds or cost more than $2,000. So the problem of the gas tank went unfixed. Ford's legal department did a risk analysis (using more metrics to justify the metrics) and concluded that with the number of accidents they could anticipate, it was cheaper to pay off the families of the people who were immolated than it was to do a recall and fix all the gas tanks. They assigned specific dollar amounts to human life and to types of burn injuries.

The Ford executives separated the analysis from the big-picture view that included ethics. From a financial point of view, the conclusion made short-term sense. The conflicting need of long-term consequences was completely neglected.

When the Pinto's gas tanks did explode in accidents, Ford asked victims and their families for secrecy. There was the prospect of a big payday as long as there was no trial or publicity.

Temporarily leaving the ethical component of the decision aside, they failed to account for the fact that large numbers of people cannot be expected to keep a secret. Compound that probability with the reality that you may have a disgruntled employee or someone in the know who has an attack of conscience, and the secret is out instantly. Compound that with the fact that there are government employees whose entire job is investigating the proliferation of certain types of accidents and you can only conclude that the people at Ford who made the decision to distribute the flawed cars were complete idiots. And then, there's the jury. What do they do when they find out the company knew about the problem and ignored it?

Ford got killed both pragmatically and ethically. They had to do the recall anyway—although it didn't occur until after the car had been on the road a decade—so it turns out that the ethical decision would have actually been the cheaper one.

The Ford executives faced a range of possibilities, not just "fix it and move on to producing a safe, if slightly more expensive, car" versus "don't fix it and move on to the inevitable payoffs." That range of possibilities had to do with how much influence each department held in the company, the dollar value of the competitive threats from other car manufacturers in the small car market, the track record of the engineering division in delivering on promises versus that of the legal department, the ego of the CEO, and much more. As you can see, the possibilities were a mix of either/or and both/and relationships that could not become clear with the metrics-driven approach to evaluating options.

Like the Ford Pinto, many projects are ill-fated; in fact, the widely reported estimate of project failure is 70 percent. The reason they earn the designation "failure" is because one or more of the so-called Triple Constraints of project management has been violated—that is, the project did not come in on time and/or on budget and/or it did not meet performance requirements. The outcomes are projects like the Leaning Tower of Pisa, the collapse of Vietnam's Can Tho Bridge during construction, and Microsoft's attempt to compete with the latest Android and Apple operating systems.

Look at the big picture encompassing your key pairs of opposites first, then list projects as action steps, and then plan and evaluate the projects with certain measurements in mind—the alternative a "tail wagging the dog" approach.

Exercise: Identifying Useful Metrics and Indicators for Risk in Your Situation

What are the metrics that tell you that you've started generating negative outcomes due to an over-focusing on one part of a paradox? These are indicators that you are starting to walk on shaky ground! They help you predict disaster and avert it.

10. Focusing on the left side of your model, determine the indicators that would signal when negative outcomes are beginning to surface.

11. Focusing on the right side of your model, determine the indicators that would signal when negative outcomes are beginning to surface.

12. Once identified, zero in on the key measures, keeping in mind industry-specific tools.

To get started, consider the many internal, external, and industry-specific evaluation tools that are standard and check off those you have used at some point.

Internal

- Exit interviews with employees.
- Customer surveys.
- Employee complaints.
- Employee performance evaluations.
- Time sheets.
- Accident reports.
- Error reports.
- Summary of accomplishments report.
- Dashboards: human resources, recruiting, sales, operations, security, information technology, project management, customer relationship management, sustainability.
- Accounting-based performance measures.
- Performance prism.

External

- Stock price.
- Gross revenue.
- Net profit margin.
- One-year sales growth.
- One-year net income growth.
- Industry analysts reports (for example, Standard & Poor's).
- Media coverage.
- Award criteria.

- Net Promoter Score (customer loyalty).
- FTSE4Good.

Industry Specific
- Press Ganey reports.
- Gartner Vendor Rating.
- Gartner Staffing Metrics.
- Manufacturing Enterprise Solutions Association (MESA) Performance Metrics.
- Bestseller lists.

Putting Metrics in the Model

Another way to think of metrics is as indicators of risk and mismanagement of the interdependent pair that makes up a paradox. Over-focusing on one side to the neglect of the other by over-committing resources to an action on one side would be an example of mismanagement.

The model template—inspired by the work of Barry Johnson—is complete with the addition of applicable metrics. See pages 174 and 175.

In working with IPC The Hospitalist Company, a leading physician group practice company focused on the delivery of hospitalist medicine and related facility-based services, I took them through all the stages of building their model. The IPC story is explored in detail in Chapter 8, but here I want to point out what the senior team led by René Toledo, executive director of the Chicago Region, determined were key metrics that would tell them whether or not they were successful in pursuing a venture into post-acute care services while they continued to support their acute-care services.

These are useful metrics expressed in their own words—still a draft, with no concern for whether any particular measurement was given a formal label. You don't need that level of formality to make the model a fully functional tool.

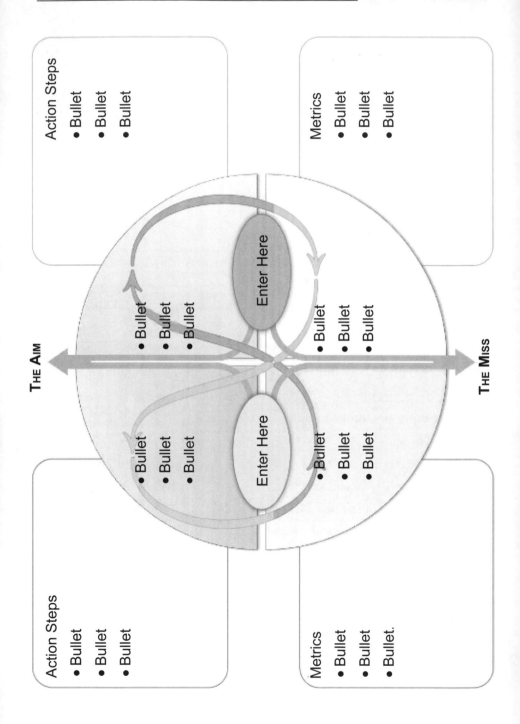

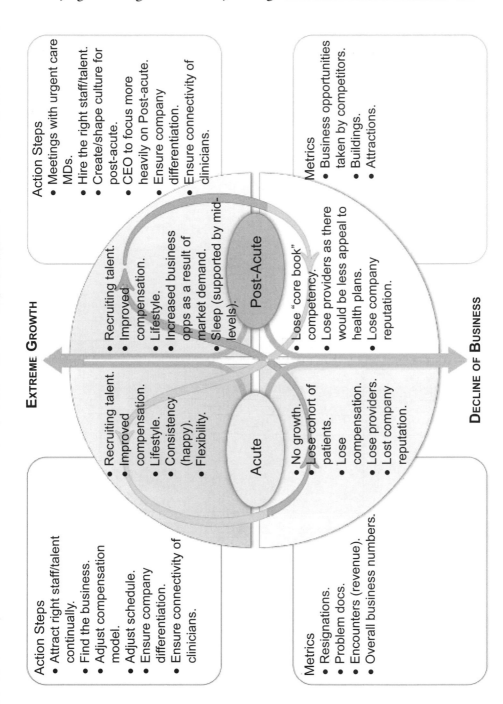

EXTREME GROWTH

DECLINE OF BUSINESS

Action Steps
- Meetings with urgent care MDs.
- Hire the right staff/talent.
- Create/shape culture for post-acute.
- CEO to focus more heavily on Post-acute.
- Ensure company differentiation.
- Ensure connectivity of clinicians.

Metrics
- Business opportunities taken by competitors.
- Buildings.
- Attractions.

Action Steps
- Attract right staff/talent continually.
- Find the business.
- Adjust compensation model.
- Adjust schedule.
- Ensure company differentiation.
- Ensure connectivity of clinicians.

Metrics
- Resignations.
- Problem docs.
- Encounters (revenue).
- Overall business numbers.

Post-Acute
- Recruiting talent.
- Improved compensation.
- Lifestyle.
- Increased business opps as a result of market demand.
- Sleep (supported by mid-levels).
- Lose "core book" competency.
- Lose providers as there would be less appeal to health plans.
- Lose company reputation.

Acute
- Recruiting talent.
- Improved compensation.
- Lifestyle.
- Consistency (happy).
- Flexibility.
- No growth.
- Lose cohort of patients.
- Lose compensation.
- Lose providers.
- Lost company reputation.

Action Plan				
THE AIM: Today's date:				
Action Steps (What Needs to Be Done)	Resources Needed (Money/ Time/People)	Measurement	Target Date	Status
Risks:				

Models help companies "unpack" their situation: take everything out of the suitcase and lay it out in an organized fashion. They help you see exactly what you have and make it clearer than it was before what the organization might be missing. You "repack" when you go operational with the content of the models.

This is where the action plan comes into play. (A sample form is provided on page 176.)

An action plan is still considered a draft of what you intend to do, but it puts your information in a form that makes it workable for the organization. The template represented here is an example; companies often want to use their own version. Use whatever your organization relies on to go operational with the information. It "repacks" what you had in the models.

Chapter 8

Respecting Context and Complexity

"The elements of a system may
themselves be systems, and every system
may be part of a larger system."[1]
—Russell Ackoff

Throughout Part I, the many references to the importance of "context" were meant as a reminder that any plans you make or actions you take are done within a universe affected by economics, politics, operational/technical factors, and social interactions. Inside of that universe is the pervasive culture of your own organization. Never lose sight of these contextual factors as you implement the process of applying paradox thinking to your problem-solving.

The Importance of Context

To drive home the point of context, I want to call out some disastrous business decisions and then look at a few success stories. In each of the first two failure situations described, it would have been virtually impossible for company executives to get the action steps right—or even identify central paradoxes—because they ignored their context.

Eastman Kodak developed the first digital camera in 1975. If senior executives had possessed foresight that was even a fraction of our hindsight, they would have tried to manage the paradox innovation *and* consistency. But not looking at the broad context in which digital technologies were developing put Kodak at a distinct disadvantage as it drew up plans and committed resources to its popular photographic film products. Microsoft was born in 1975. IBM introduced bar-code scanners in 1974. Commodore and Atari were getting their computers into homes in the mid-1970s. With all of that consumer-oriented digital activity going on in the 1970s and then continuing to build each year, how did Kodak's senior executives miss the signs for more than 15 years, then finally take action to join the crowd? In all likelihood, even if Kodak executives had thought in terms of paradoxes in the late 1970s, they would have all centered on conflicting needs within the photographic film business and still missed the opportunity they needed to pursue in order to avert bankruptcy years later.

MSN Money's Jason Nolte didn't hold back in his June 12, 2013, article assessing how Sears executives failed to see the business world around them. In "Why Americans Hate Sears," he said, "They hate it as a place to shop. They hate it as an investment. They hate that it hasn't changed so much as a doorknob or drop-ceiling tile in 20 years."[2] The problems belong jointly to Sears and Kmart; the latter bought Sears in 2005, sharing their tragic myopia about American retail. In a period when competitors were hiring top design experts to arrange bath towels in a way that invited shoppers to move directly to pricier items, Sears and Kmart tinkered with logos and made some changes in shelf height. They spent $1 to $2 per square foot on updating facilities, whereas Target and Wal-Mart committed $8 and more per square foot. And at a time when competitors invested in new tools to manage their supply chain, the Kmart-Sears team clung to their old technology as tightly as they did their old ceiling tiles.

Looking at the context in which Sears and Kmart operate, an important part of the environment is a social issue as much as it is an operational or economic one. Successful retailers know that a great store offers an enjoyable experience, with both ambience and customer service. Lack of both cannot be fixed by being among the top 20 advertisers in the nation.[3] The paradox has three parts, all of which become clearest when the business is viewed in context: efficiency *and* attention to customer needs/desires *and* advertising.

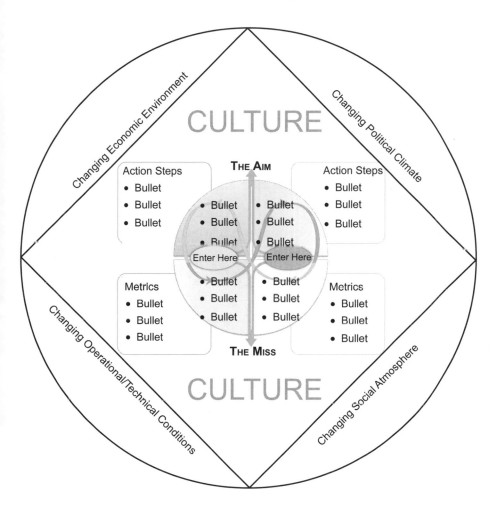

The final negative scenario comes from something a literary agent told me. If you think of authors as entrepreneurs—businesses of one—then you acknowledge that their understanding of context is just as important as it is for Kodak or Sears, or any other entrepreneur. Unfortunately, many of them believe so much in their product and talent that they ignore the environment in which they hope to operate (sound familiar?). They generally don't think of the political aspect of publishing, with biases abounding, or the operational constraints that publishers have to manage. They don't bother to analyze how the economic climate affects their chances of getting published or how much money the company may be able—not just willing—to provide as an advance. The one aspect of the context they do tend to see is the social climate—that this, the importance of the connectedness of author to agent and agent to publisher. As an agent, she tries to school authors about the whole context, not just one-quarter of it. And like many companies that go out of business quickly, those who ignore context are unable to manage the paradoxes that lead to success—for example, marketing *and* editorial quality, efficiency *and* attention to detail, confidence *and* responsiveness.

In contrast, Ameren Corporation's awareness of context actually drove it away from managing a central paradox of its business operation and into an either/or choice. The energy company had functioned as both a regulated and a deregulated business, but in 2012, the decision was made to go back to the core business, which is regulated, and move out of the deregulated arena. Leadership looked at the energy industry landscape and estimated total value benefits associated with a divestiture of its deregulated business at $900 million.

Divesting the deregulated arm of the business positions Ameren "as a company focused exclusively on its rate-regulated electric, natural gas and transmission operations, clarifying our strategic direction and value proposition to investors,"[4] according to company chairman Thomas R. Voss. The reasons he cited for the move were to reduce business risk and improve the predictability of the company's future earnings and cash flows. The ancillary effects would be to strengthen Ameren's credit profile and support the company's dividend.

Another positive story of understanding context comes out of a Midwestern town and centers on a small not-for-profit group. For two years, Nancy served as president of this charitable organization made up solely of volunteers who raise money for educational programs. She guided her group into unprecedented fundraising success by asking them to stop saying, "We could do this, or we could do that." For the first time in the group's history, they sought grant money from a local source instead of relying solely on grassroots fundraising.

Nancy determined the group was capable doing the both/and approach for two reasons related to context. She had seen the community both as a volunteer with other organizations and as a bank employee. For that reason, she had a somewhat different perspective on the context in which the organization operated than did many of her fellow volunteers. She knew these things:

- The economic situation of the community in general was sound.
- A very high percentage of local people seemed inclined toward charitable giving.
- Neighborly behavior was valued, and even professionals were willing to donate their skills and time in a commitment to be neighborly.
- Technology, event space, and other physical resources were commonly made available to charities by local businesses.

Other groups in town doing related kinds of charitable work were—without exception—either/or groups: Either they were composed of people who were wealthy and wrote big checks, or they were all-grassroots organizations. None of them effectively leveraged the talents and resources associated with operating in the context of this particular community. Her logic is simply this: *When I am faced with a situation in which I have two options, I look at what's good about option A and what's good about option B. And then I ask myself, "Can they work in tandem?"*

Her most aggressive paradox proposal as the group's leader was to suggest the group simultaneously establish a small foundation that they wouldn't touch until they had amassed $5,000, and to continue to funnel money directly to individual students and institutions they had selected as recipients. She introduced a roomful of very fearful people—volunteers who thought this scheme would put them way over their heads and tie up funds for years that they should be giving away tomorrow—by talking about the average banking customer at her branch. A person with $5,000 doesn't want to set up a money market account because he can write only three checks a year, so he decides to put everything into a checking account. The bank professional's job is to point out that the best option is to open two accounts and write a check from the money market account to seed the checking account. It wasn't a precise analogy, but it did get people in the room thinking about short-term *and* long-term needs as expressed by foundation *and* immediate funding.

It's important for a leader to pay attention to how others are succeeding in the same context. The paradox in this not-for-profit scenario is my way *and* your way. Identifying sources of quality, alternative thinking—and then listening to them—are great action steps for virtually any paradox model!

LinkedIn's growth and development initiatives also reflect a keen grasp of context. Borne into the mix of social media ventures, LinkedIn at first seemed to be all about the numbers: Become part of a growing world of interconnected professionals. The mission seemed to be to join LinkedIn and then connect with as many other professionals in related fields as possible. But for what end? During its early years, LinkedIn seemed to be a junk pile of CVs and resumes. And then after the recession hit in 2008, LinkedIn leadership seemed to enrich their understanding of the critical importance of context. Its members were focused on networking for a purpose; they had goals of career development, professional opportunities, landing a job.

▶ The changing environment meant chaotic economic conditions.

- The changing political climate involved loss of leaders, replacement of managers, personnel holes in the organizational structure.

- The changing operational/technical conditions reflected new procedures, including new hiring procedures that were reliant on technology, and upgrades to improve efficiency and cut costs.

- The changing social atmosphere was a mixture of generations in the workforce that was unprecedented.

Armed with this understanding of their context, LinkedIn's leadership transitioned from one more social media network to this:

> In the past year LinkedIn has emerged as one of the most powerful business tools on the planet. Long considered a repository for digital résumés, the network now reports 225 million members who have set up profiles and uploaded their education and job histories. These days they're doing far more than prospecting for new gigs. LinkedIn users are building professional portfolios that showcase their best work, from publications to videos to PowerPoint presentation. They are relying on a growing array of LinkedIn apps, like CardMunch, which lets users scan business cards to upload contact information. They're recommending one another for particular business attributes. And increasingly they're logging on to read LinkedIn Today, which aggregates news from myriad sources. Thanks to new features like those, the number of users who log on at least once a month on desktops alone (excluding mobile) has climbed to 141 million worldwide, according to ComScore, a 37% jump over last year.
>
> Among recruiters, LinkedIn has become the standard—88 of the Fortune 100 have licensed the software to help find and track potential job candidates.[5]

As you go operational with paradox thinking, make sure you take into account the elements of your environment as they did at LinkedIn.

LinkedIn CEO Jeff Weiner clearly sees the company's context as one shaped by global factors and not just national ones. His plans to build new features and services into the network reflect that vision: "Imagine a platform that can digitally represent every opportunity in the world…. LinkedIn will provide a real-time measure of where jobs exist, where customers aren't being serviced, and where people need training."[6]

The Emergence of Complexity

When contexts and cultures clash, groups caught in the conflict face complex organizational challenges. At the heart of those challenges, you will find pairs of opposites. Common examples are businesses acquired by other organizations with very different cultures and/or representing industries operating in a different context.

Quaker Oats' disastrous acquisition of Snapple Beverage Company exemplifies what has happened in many such situations: The acquiring company imposes its perception of context and its culture on the other business. Instead of trying to leverage the distribution channels and advertising programs it had in place *and* honor the distribution network and branding that Snapple had developed so successfully, Quaker distributed and promoted Snapple the way it did the rest of its products. The interrelated and immediate results were profound. Quaker's misstep gave Coca Cola and PepsiCo an opening to compete directly against Snapple with new products. In addition, Quaker had acquired Snapple in 1994 for $1.7 billion, but sold it 27 months later for a mere $300 million.

A dramatic example of a clash of context and culture—one with sweeping ramifications for business and individuals—took the spotlight in early September 2013. It had come to light that selected government agencies, particularly the United States National Security Agency (NSA), had greater ability to penetrate corporate and personal internet security measures than private-sector computer experts had realized.

Contributions to the all-volunteer group responsible for internet security from government "volunteers" had been affected by their interest in ensuring that government could break the codes if they deemed it necessary. The question was, Could an either/or issue of protection of the citizenry *versus* corporate/individual privacy/security be managed as a pair of interdependent opposites?

The Internet Engineering Task Force (IETF) consists of thousands of people from all over the world. They do not pay fees to join the organization, but instead they gather physically and/or virtually throughout the year for meetings related to internet issues, such as how e-mail works and how internet security can be improved. They may be affiliated with companies or government agencies, or they may be unaffiliated with any organization. There are no barriers to entry; anyone with the technical savvy and desire to contribute may do so.

The system has worked extraordinarily well for decades. In the years following the attacks on the World Trade Center's Twin Towers on September 11, 2001, however, security agencies of many countries have been concerned about their ability to penetrate corporate security, as well as privacy protections available to individual people. With internal NSA documents coming to light as a result of breaches of trust such as those related to Edward Snowden[7], IETF participants became aware that their best efforts appeared to have been undermined by some of their colleagues.

IETF committee chairs seemed to gravitate immediately toward a paradox approach to the issue; government agencies did not. IETF felt that it might be in everyone's best interests to go back to the drawing board—to recognize the seemingly conflicting needs and proceed with good-faith efforts to revamp the specifications for internet security. As of this writing, it remains to be seen if paradox will trump either/or, but the forces of commerce and individual liberty support IETF's paradox approach.

The upbeat side of the complexity discussion is how to avoid it. Perhaps the most straightforward and paradox-focused explanation of how to do acquisitions and mergers to avoid a clash of context and culture has been offered by Carl Shepherd, founder of HomeAway. Even the vacation company's tagline suggests "and": "Let's stay together." Shepherd led 18 global acquisitions in an eight-year period beginning in 2005, translating to an average of more than two acquisitions per year. Prior to joining HomeAway, he served as the Hoover's Online COO and oversaw a number of acquisitions there as well.

Forbes contributor Cheryl Conner captured Shepherd's six key pieces of advice, in which managing three pairs of interdependent opposites emerges as his formula for success.[8] Shepherd advises to "court them" and "don't rely on traditional valuations." The substance of this pair is "know what they want" *and* "know what you want." He next says, "Use the best advisors you can get" and "Advise the seller to get the best advisors they can get, too." That pair needs no interpretation. Finally, Shepherd advises, "Focus on integration from day one," and "Have a plan." This is paradox of short term and long term that has found its way into nearly every company scenario.

Creating Market Advantages

Companies that have a keen understanding of their context will naturally see new market opportunities as they emerge. In my work with the Chicago Region at IPC the Hospitalist Company (IPC), it became clear in conversations with the executive director that a new opportunity was taking shape for the company because of market shifts. If the company chose to exploit it, leadership would be faced with managing a significant paradox in order to drive future growth.

IPC "is on the leading edge of a growing U.S. trend toward hospitalist specialization,"[9] according to the Hoover's analysis of the company by Anne Law. IPC provides more than 1,400 hospitalists in 28 states, and backs up the physicians with management and administrative services.

Hospitalists are healthcare providers that traditionally have focused on inpatient care and services.

The hospitalists' professional society, the Society of Hospital Medicine (SHM), has defined hospitalist as a physician whose primary professional focus (clinical, teaching, research, or administration) is general inpatient care. A hospitalist may be an employee of a hospital or HMO, a contractor, or a private practitioner. About 75 percent of hospitalists are general internists. Hospital-based primary care physicians free general practitioners from the need to make daily rounds to visit hospitalized patients. Several studies have shown significant decreases in hospital costs and in length of hospital stays under the hospitalist system, with no decline in quality of care or patient satisfaction. Some academic medical centers have adopted hospitalist models for inpatient care and teaching.[10]

Until 2013, IPC's growth strategy primarily involved three types of activities. The first was expanding its services to new institutions in areas where it already operated. The second aspect of the growth strategy involved recruiting and training additional hospitalists. The third was moving into new regions.

In early 2013, company senior executives determined that IPC faced another major—and highly time-sensitive—growth opportunity related to the "traditional" definition of hospitalist. In fact, they decided to redefine it to enter a new market. Senior executives in the Chicago Region knew that their ability to take advantage of the significant new opportunity depended a great deal on a shared understanding of options and actions company-wide. They took the plunge into paradox thinking with the intent of bringing the process to the Chicago Region staff and the Practice Group Leaders (PGL) Council, the key leaders of each practice in the Chicago Region.

Perspectives of Regional Senior Executives

EXTREME GROWTH

DECLINE OF BUSINESS

Action Steps
- Meetings with urgent care MDs
- Hire the right staff/ talent.
- Create/shape culture for post-acute.
- CEO to focus more on post-acute.
- Ensure company differentiation.
- Ensure connectivity of clinicians.

Metrics
- Business opportunities taken by competitors.
- Buildings.
- Attractions.

Post-Acute

- Recruiting talent.
- Improved compensation.
- Lifestyle.
- Increased business ops as a result of market demand.
- Sleep (supported by mid-levels.)

- Lose "core book" competency.
- Lose providers as there would be less appeal to health plans.
- Lose company reputation.

Acute

- Recruiting talent.
- Improved compensation.
- Lifestyle.
- Consistency (happy).
- Flexibility.

- No growth.
- Lose cohort of patients.
- Lose compensation.
- Lose providers.
- Lost company reputation.

Action Steps
- Attract right staff/talent continually.
- Find the business.
- Adjust compensation model.
- Adjust schedule.
- Ensure company differentiation.
- Ensure connectivity of clinicians.

Metrics
- Resignations.
- Problem docs.
- Encounters (revenue).
- Overall business numbers.

The opportunity was summed up in the paradox acute (core focus) *and* post-acute (new focus). Post-acute is the medical term describing the care a patient receives after discharge from a hospital. It can involve a rehabilitation facility, assisted living, skilled nursing, and so on, and it can serve patients of any age—from newborns with special medical needs to elderly patients recovering after a hospitalization.

The triad of senior executives who first worked with me to capture the paradox and model all aspects of it is quite different in terms of thinking preferences. (Refer to Chapter 3 and the discussion of HBDI.) It was interesting to see how the strengths and predispositions of each actually complemented each other as we developed the original map for acute *and* post-acute.

Please note that I consider it very important for engagement of the participants to use their language rather than impose some kind of standard nomenclature on them. Yes, the model may appear rough and some of the information indiscernible to "outsiders," but it helps move the process forward; it supports a team in going operational with paradox thinking. The senior executives' model is the one cited in Chapter 7, which highlighted the metrics contained therein.

Before plunging into narrative analysis of the differences and similarities between the executives' model and those of the staff and practice leaders, consider the models they created in their team sessions.

The three teams worked on the models featured on pages 190, 192, and 193 independently, which is why they overlap and the convergence of input is so interesting. Despite the differences in word choice, the positive and negative outcomes, action steps, and metrics are remarkably similar. The teams were close on citing how to go about achieving positive outcomes, and what kind of numbers and results they needed to stay aware of that would signal over-focus on one part of the paradox at the neglect of the other. The most significant difference in style of expression—but not salient content—comes from the PGL Council, who are physicians operating in clinical environments.

Perspectives of Chicago Region Staff

EXTREME GROWTH ←→ **DECLINE OF BUSINESS**

Action Steps

- Hire the right talent on the team.
- Get into more buildings.
- Refine the model (needing consistency on metrics).
- Must have requirements of model.
- Be prepared for new competitors.

Metrics

- # Encounters.
- # New buildings.
- # Providers (inability to hire new providers).

Action Steps

- Hire fit talent for the future.
- Get more business (buildings, referrals, etc.).
- Refine PGL pool.
- Improve patient satisfaction.
- Differentiate!
- Explore 7-on7-off schedule.

Metrics

- # Encounters.
- # New buildings.
- # Providers (inability to hire new providers).

Post-Acute

Acute

- Major growth.
- Visibility.
- Seize the market.
- Positive relationships with hospitals.

- Employee engagement.
- Stability.
- Improved financial performance.
- Visibility.
- Positive relationships with hospitals/groups.

- Lose acute business.
- Lose post-acute business.
- Put IPC-Chicago at risk.
- Radically changes our identity.

- Reduced post-acute revenue.
- Lose providers.
- Put IPC-Chicago at risk.
- Lose appeal to health plans.

Perspectives of PGL Council

GROW THE CHICAGO REGION

Action Steps

- Look at "presence" in both. Need to sustain.
- Have everyone learn the "recipe" as we grow in other buildings. Mentoring on IPC Way is a good approach for this.
- Staffing.
- Act fast before competition sees.
- Look at models/be creative.

Action Steps

- Staffing (we need enough; need the right staffing, need to retain staff, need to look at models/be creative).
- Definitive strategy to maintain and grow.
- Differentiators (answering the phones, presence, quality, etc.).
- Engagement (get partners involved; need to be engaged).
- Leadership (common vision).

SLOW DEATH FOR CHICAGO REGION

Metrics

- # Growth rate (slows).
- # Clinical metrics (start to deteriorate).
- # Hiring (challenges here).

Metrics

- # Volume—revenue decrease.
- # Hospitals (start hiring on their own; emergence of competition).
- # Resignations (increase).
- # Referrals from post-acute (decrease).

Post-Acute

Acute

- Recruiting talent.
- Improved compensation.
- Lifestyle.
- Increased business opps as a result of market demand.
- Sleep (supported by mid-levels).

- Secure business.
- Ability to grow.
- Quality and quantity.
- Uniformity/ standardization.
- Attractive to others.
- Attractive to post-acute.

- Wouldn't be honest.
- Less referrals.
- Less volume of patients.
- Less appeal to payers.

- Watch the bus go by.
- Less jobs/less opportunity.
- Continuity of care interrupted.
- Less appealing to acute.
- Inability to refer to ourselves.

Key commonalities include the strategies to hire and retain talent, to maintain and increase the number of facilities where IPC provides services, and to manage provider relationships. Corresponding metrics appear in all three models; for example, failure to retain talent is seen in the number of resignations. This kind of compatibility is far more than a coincidence. It's a reflection of clear communication from leadership of hospitalist opportunities in the Chicago marketplace.

Ultimately, the first actions taken that correspond to those listed to support "acute" included adjusting the way that new physicians are hired, reconfiguring their compensation packages, and implementing new measures to retain current doctors. They took complementary actions listed to become competitive in the post-acute arena. The process of both implementing action steps and keeping an eye on metrics continues as IPC Chicago pursues new ventures in the post-acute market.

IPC's Chicago Region operates in two contexts: the greater Chicago area and its own national organization. The different teams who built the models focused squarely on the Aim and the Miss related to their region and what they needed to do to exploit their opportunity to move into an emerging area of business—that is, post-acute. Not every region of IPC faced the same opportunity to move into post-acute in the near-term, however, so IPC's national leadership needed to manage the paradox of centralized _and_ decentralized, allowing Chicago to take initiative some other regions were not taking. They needed to balance making decisions out of corporate office, but ensuring autonomy for IPC Chicago so it could extend its services to a post-acute market that was clearly growing.

The Hoover's analysis spotlights another paradox faced by the national organization that national leadership is balancing well—that is, acquisitions _and_ organic growth: "In addition to its main growth strategy of acquiring existing practice groups in new markets, IPC strives to offer its services to new institutions in areas where it already operates."[11]

Nested in this set of objectives is IPC's acknowledgment that administrative and clinical leadership need to be balanced in order to meet customers' requirements in this ever-changing world of healthcare. In other words, business and patient care have to have equal billing for the company to achieve its Aim.

Respect the context wherein you operate and the culture that enables you to thrive in that context. If your group is part of a larger organization, make it clear to your national/global leadership why your context demands that you exploit or avoid specific market opportunities.

PART III

Results of
Implementing
the
Process

Chapter 9

Going Operational

"Life can only be understood backward,
but it must be lived forward."
—Sjoren Kierkagaard

The process of using paradox thinking "unpacks" a company's situation—and that shows up in the rough development of the models. After that, the process involves a "repacking" as you translate the final model into an action plan with objectives, sequence, time line, accountability, and goals.

At the Beginning of the Process

Max and Colleen Starkloff founded Paraquad in 1970. It is a nonprofit organization whose mission is to empower people with disabilities to increase their independence through choice and opportunity. With their focus on their home of St. Louis, they put an emphasis on community involvement supported by grassroots fundraising. The section "About Paraquad" on the organization's Website notes services to its home community of St. Louis, even though Max Starkloff pioneered adaptations such as the cut-outs for wheelchairs in sidewalks that can now be seen all over the country.

Though Max was the face and "soul" of the organization throughout his 33 years of leadership, it became clear that the organization would benefit from complementary talent. There needed to be diverse expertise and different ways of approaching business issues. The first CEO at Paraquad after Max stepped down emphasized securing grants and had tremendous success, growing the annual operating budget from $4 million to $11 million in an 11-year period. With shifts in the economic climate after the recession that began in 2008, attracting grant money became a much more challenging proposition. That uphill struggle continued for a few years. In the meantime, some pools of contributions that had been associated with a more grassroots model had not been cultivated; these funds no longer flowed into Paraquad. When I entered into discussions with Paraquad, that was the situation they faced.

Many great plans were taking shape, such as a one-of-a kind recreation and fitness facility designed to enable people with and without disabilities to work out together. Programs generating fees, such as "home care and attendant services," vocational rehabilitation, employment counseling, and so on, were becoming more robust. In order to achieve such major projects, as well as continue supporting smaller success stories, the organization needed a combination of approaches to broaden its base of income sources. I met with the marketing executive for Paraquad and created the following map shown on page 201—the first draft of the model to help Paraquad to go operational with paradox thinking.

The model is a first draft. It's isn't "perfect," and that's precisely the reason why it appears here. It captures enough relevant and interrelated information that it allowed Paraquad to proceed in tackling their development challenge. Similarly, as you launch your efforts to address seemingly conflicting needs, put the thoughts of your team into the model without excessive attention to word choice or cross-checking the positive and negatives outcomes as described in Chapter 6.

BROAD BASE OF DIVERSE INCOME SOURCES

FINANCIAL VULNERABILITY

Action Steps
- Build awareness through events and awards program.
- Start a young professionals group.
- Initiate friend-raisers.
- Cause-based marketing.
- Provide good stewardship.

Metrics
- Lack of community awareness.
- Loss of brand identity.
- Fee for services not growing; referral relationship decreasing.

Grants-Fundraising

- Establish relationship with funders for long term.
- Sustainable and long-term individual donors.
- Find volunteers.
- Can start small, grow, stay.

- Vulnerable (funders change philosophy, we can't replace).
- Vulnerable because of changes in economic conditions.
- Losing ground to competition for fees.

- Big-ticket items paid for.
- Build relationship with corporate entities.
- Funding for specific programs.

Fee for Services Programming

- Reliance on government payments
- Individual donors dry up.
- Constantly looking for new customers.

Action Steps
- Write a good case—outcome based.
- Conduct benchmarking studies.
- Advertising decisions (consumers and/or partners).

Metrics
- Decrease of donors.
- Decrease in forecast.
- Increasing commercial competition.

In the Middle of the Process

Shrades (a real company I have masked with a different name) began life as an insurance brokerage and financial services firm in 1937. I would describe it as a highly individualistic holding company. With a quick look at the Website, the emphasis on "distinguishing character-istics and core values" is clear. For this company, managing paradoxes means both making money for their clients and always maintaining the values established decades ago that shape their business practices.

Headquartered in New York, the company maintains locations around the globe and is made up of about 1,200 employees, 25 percent of whom have ownership in the firm. Its current numbers are the tip of the success story; the portion "below the surface" is that a history of success that has enabled the company to be consistently profitable.

- Capital $352 million, as of March 31, 2012.
- Revenues $491 million for fiscal 2012.
- Total assets under management $77.3 billion, as of March 31, 2013.

Many individual businesses comprise the Shrades portfolio, so a key strategic concern was having metrics in place to determine how those businesses are performing—to have a system of ascertaining if each individual business was still enjoying mid-day sunshine or fading into the dusk of its corporate life. The leadership of Shrades took steps to determine that, but many factors related to the company's values seemed to get in the way. In short, the evaluative process wasn't simple. It wasn't just about numbers indicating performance; it was also about supporting the people leading and working for those businesses.

Shrades lived a paradox: Culturally, it was the kind of company that had loyalty to its clients, as evidenced by strong returns, and the kind of company that had loyalty to its people, as evidenced by employee reten-tion and significant employee ownership. Company leadership found it much easier to talk about common shared values and how businesses aligned to values, rather than to scrutinize performance and make hard decisions related to bad performance. At the same time, Shrades leadership knew that company executives and heads of the individuals businesses had to have the hard conversations about performance.

I walked into Shrades "in the middle of things." What had occurred was acknowledgment that a transition in culture and operational practices had begun. The paradox Shrades defined as its focus is individual businesses *and* shared businesses—that is, aligned and integrated businesses. Other possible conflicts are nested in the latter, which involves shared decision-making about the different businesses *and* individual business leaders participating in corporate decisions *and* individual business leaders making discrete decisions. Another complicating factor woven into the paradox on both sides is that some of the businesses rely on intellectual property that is shared with other Shrades companies. The extent to which a company is an "individual business" might be mitigated by how much it relied on that shared IP.

The positive outcomes of focusing on individual business are that each is able to create and maximize a sustainable and profitable portion of its market, to establish uniqueness in its market, and to maintain a competitive edge.

The negative outcomes of over-focusing on the individual business are that many leaders would be capable of guiding their own enterprises, but that could jeopardize the ability to guide and coordinate the whole portfolio. Another negative is that insufficient attention would be paid to whether or not all the businesses in the portfolio were even the right ones. Even with its history of consistent profitability, Shrades leadership knew there had to be times when some of the businesses in the portfolio were underperforming, yet they remained part of the company. This is easily a negative outcome if a respect for the autonomy of individual business supersedes attention to the overall corporate mission. A third negative outcome is loss of opportunities across the businesses; there would be little or no cross-pollination.

A key upside of focusing on aligned and integrated businesses is the development of leaders who have the ability to see beyond their own business and involve themselves in shared decision-making in the direction of the firm. As a corollary, another positive outcome is the cultivation of objective decision-making about the individual business; if the leaders of those business have concern for the company as a whole as part of their thinking, they are likely to look at each decision from multiple angles. There is also the potential for synergies such as cross-selling.

The major negative outcomes of over-focusing on aligned and integrated business are not being agile or responsive to individual markets, and having the businesses become diluted—that is, a loss of uniqueness.

Shrades's Aim in managing the paradox well is wealth creation for clients, with the Miss being continuing to carry people out of loyalty to business. Keep in mind that the Miss does not signify a company backing away from its values, but rather facing a reality that some individuals, and some individual businesses, are not contributors. For any number of reasons, they become a drag on profit and it is not reasonable to keep them out of some artificial loyalty.

Action steps for focus on the individual businesses are:

▶ Make tough decisions about businesses going from the expansion stage to the mature stage. These stages, described in Chapter 3, have certain paradoxes associated with them. The "tough decisions" that Shrades would have to make could therefore be centered on the extent to which a business was managing all or most of the paradoxes associated with the expansion stage. That is:

  ◆ Current products/services *and* complementary products/services.

  ◆ Organic growth *and* acquisitive growth.

  ◆ Local footprint *and* national/global footprint.

  ◆ Entrepreneurial spirit *and* adherence to the need for systematic and regulated growth.

▶ Spot market opportunity.

▶ Codify skill sets of leaders.

▶ When time to get out, improve identification of target market and segments, and focus on those.

▶ Acquire and develop talent internally, not just externally.

Actions steps on aligned and integrated businesses are:

▶ Develop governance around the sense of ownership of the firm as a whole.

▶ Improve the process for collecting, analyzing, and making decisions based on data.

▶ Create a portfolio process for the business.

▶ Configure a more appropriate resource allocation system.

▶ Put a succession plan in place.

Metrics indicating you are in negative territory in terms of focusing on individual businesses include three clear internal and one clear external measurement. The internal metrics include:

1. No CEO succession candidate.

2. A lack of transparency in terms of seeing interrelatedness of businesses and performance evaluations of the businesses.

3. A lack of participation by individual business leaders in questioning and scrutinizing performance of the company as a whole.

The external metric is straightforward: the profitability of the company drops.

Metrics indicating they are getting negative outcomes as a result of over-focusing on aligned and integrated business include a lack of entrepreneurship and reduced willingness to take risks, a lacking strategy for operation ten years down the road and a plan for how to get there, and the lack of a sustainable process for growing the company.

As plotted on a map the assembled perspectives look like this:

WEALTH CREATION FOR CLIENTS

CARRYING PEOPLE OUT OF LOYALTY

Shared Businesses

Individual Businesses

Action Steps
- Develop governance around sense of ownership of firm.
- Improve process to collect, analyze, decide based on data.
- Create portfolio process for business.
- Improve resource allocation.
- Put a success plan in place.

Metrics
- Lack of entrepreneurship.
- Reduced willingness to take risks.
- Lacking strategy for operation 10 years down the road.
- Lack of sustainable process for growing the company.

Shared Businesses perspectives:
- Development of leaders with big-picture view.
- Cultivation of objective decision-making about the individual businesses.
- Potential for synergies, such as cross-selling.

- Losing agility.
- Becoming less responsive to individual markets.
- Loss of uniqueness.

Individual Businesses perspectives:
- Each can create/maximize a sustainable and profitable portion of its market.
- Each can establish uniqueness in its market.
- Each can maintain a competitive edge.

- Jeopardize ability to coordinate whole porfolio.
- Insufficient attention to whether all businesses in portfolio were the right ones.
- Loss of opps across businesses; little or no cross-polination.

Action Steps
- Make tough decisions about businesses going from expansion stage to mature stage.
- Spot market opportunity.
- Codify skill sets of leaders.
- Improve ID of target markets.
- Develop talent internally and externally.

Metrics
- No CEO succession candidate.
- Lack of transparency vis a vis businesses and performance evaluations of businesses.
- Lack of participation by individual business leaders in questioning performance of company as a whole.
- Corporate profitability drops.

Seeing Results

Livli Hotels, discussed in Chapter 1 and Chapter 3, began with its human resources team identifying key paradoxes and working on maps. One of the goals they surfaced in the from-to exercise I led was the desire to move from a situation where they pushed ideas at senior executives to one where they were being invited to present ideas and take actions; they felt that helping the organization achieve priority objectives meant that they had to be proactive and strategic with corporate leaders. The shift started to occur because of their efforts to adopt paradox thinking. Liz P., the executive vice president for human resources, presented the models her team had created in a senior staff meeting. Her fellow executives and the CEO were riveted. With clarity and specificity, they saw how the core challenge of focusing on both their global and their local presence captured the way forward. The executives discussed "global and local" in light of the CEO's four stated priorities and concluded that it was a foundational consideration to:

1. Grow profitably.
2. Innovate in the area of guest services.
3. Build organizational capability.
4. Stay ahead in developing key markets.

Liz brought some models that were HR-specific so the executives could see how her team hoped to manage paradoxes that supported the overarching "global and local" sets of needs. The big picture of global *and* local was also covered in a map that might be called a draft #1 model. It contained sufficient detail and analysis that senior executives had confidence in initiating some of the action steps.

The HR-specific maps primarily covered topics related to creating "more tools for capability building," which also came out of the from-to exercise. For example, one Aim was retaining key talent, and the central portion of the map looked like this:

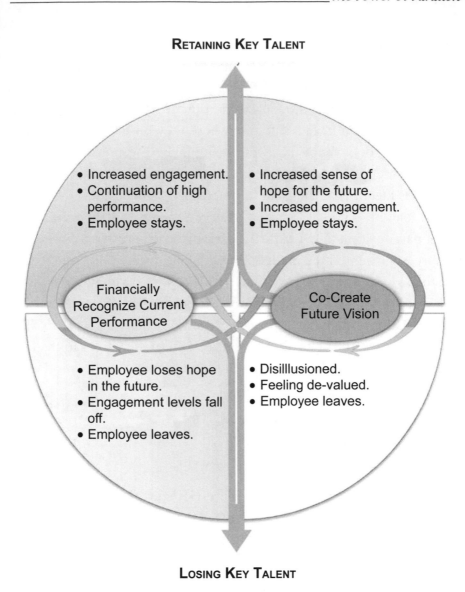

RETAINING KEY TALENT

- Increased engagement.
- Continuation of high performance.
- Employee stays.

- Increased sense of hope for the future.
- Increased engagement.
- Employee stays.

Financially Recognize Current Performance

Co-Create Future Vision

- Employee loses hope in the future.
- Engagement levels fall off.
- Employee leaves.

- Disilllusioned.
- Feeling de-valued.
- Employee leaves.

LOSING KEY TALENT

The HR team's initial "global and local" map looked like this:

Action Steps
- Research on competing properties in the markets.
- Research on local goods/ suppliers.
- Staff and guest ideas on localizing.

Metrics
- Increased borrowing; increased need for investors.
- Outdated practices and systems.
- Customer complaints.
- Loss of opportunity to service truly global customer.

INCREASED REVENUES

REVENUE DECLINE

Local Customization
- Local décor.
- Local menu offerings.
- Local staff.
- Limited financial growth.
- Lack of standardization in level of services.
- Isolated from best practice knowledge.

Global Brand
- Consumer confidence in consistent services.
- Speed through integrated systems.
- Shared best practices across the global footprint.
- Customers dissatisfied with service delivered.
- Customers choosing not to go there, décor not comfortable.
- Menu options don't meet local tastes.

Action Steps
- Codifying service offerings.
- Building communication system and protocal across chain.
- Hiring standards.

Metrics
- Drop in market share in key markets.
- Increased costs.
- Customer complaints.
- Increase of local competition.

Executives left the meeting with the CEO directing the various departments to conduct the needed research; consolidate policy documents on housekeeping, customer service, and other practices; and launch an outreach project to get ideas on localizing properties from both staff and guests. The latter would be revision and expansion of the existing practice of collecting guest feedback on performance and areas needing improvement.

The deadline they established for completing the action steps was the end of the second quarter, which was five months away. At that time, they decided to reconvene as a group and, with the assistance of our consulting group, analyze the results and built a new "master model" reflecting the next set of action steps and metrics.

Ultimately, at both the corporate and individual property levels, Livli Hotels infused staff with the concept of global and local. It differentiated them markedly from other upscale hotels that were their prime competition. One by one, keeping an eye on the metrics, properties got the go-ahead to start making changes in décor, cuisine, and dress to localize properties externally and to extend the autonomy of general managers in terms of their business interactions with local suppliers, among other things. Concurrently, they disseminated upgraded materials describing performance standards and set best practices in place. They also established a more transparent and consistent compensation program. One of the first visible examples of change was in their Taipei, Taiwan property. Each room now contained a large framed photo taken at the Taipei Zoo instead of the generic art that decorated many competitors' properties. Each guest also received the gift of a small teapot with an image of "Grandpa Lin Wang," a legendary Asian elephant that had been the most popular animal at the zoo—and perhaps the most famous in Taiwan—for many years. The addition of such seemingly small differentiators increased the appeal of the property. One of the warning signs of going into negative territory of "local" was "higher costs not covered by revenue increases." At this property, they did not see that happening; in fact, after the initial capital investments, revenue outstripped expenditures by an increased margin.

In a further effort to link general managers (GMs) and their staff with corporate thinking, each GM was asked to create and maintain a "global and local" map that captured positive and negative outcomes, action steps, and metrics for his or her individual property.

Done well, the models give an instant picture of the goal, strategy, and tactics related to a particular issue. Practically speaking, a model is a blueprint for balancing the pursuit of two seemingly conflicting objectives at the same time.

Chapter 10

Success (and Failure) Stories

"Who would have thought that Fannie
Mae would beat companies like GE
and Coca-Cola? Or that Walgreens
could beat Intel? The surprising list—a
dowdier group would be hard to find—
taught us a key lesson right up front. It
is possible to turn good into great in the
most unlikely of situations."[1]
—Jim Collins, *Good to Great*

Depending on your criteria for evaluating a company's merits, just
about any company could be defined as a success story. Even a bank-
rupt company could be viewed as an emotional success story if the
employees were "doing what they loved."

In this chapter, I hold to a more stringent definition of success, and
it revolves around a single word: sustainability. To determine the sustainability of a company, many of the metrics cited in Chapter 7 come
into play; they help determine how well a company is doing in managing certain key interdependent pairs. None alone gives the complete
picture of a company's performance, however.

There are a number of places we can look to determine which companies have achieved sustainability. Many of these same sources also give us insights into analyzing the failure to succeed; namely, they help us determine which companies *seemed* to have achieved long-term success, but somehow, ended up with the Miss rather than the Aim. In the context of a discussion on success stories, it's just as important to look at those failed companies and wonder: Do we see any of the same tendencies in the company that appear to be at the top of their game right now? The discussion also includes a few companies that suggest sustainability. That is, they appear to be on the track to managing key paradoxes well, effecting the kind of balance in leadership, organization, culture, and so on, that gives them the ability to sustain success over the long term.

A "Great" Launching Point

Jim Collins named 11 companies as having transitioned from good to great in his 2001 book *Good to Great* and based that judgment on seven characteristics. They reflect some surprise insights gleaned from the five years of research done by Collins and his team, as well as some of his long-time thinking about what lies at the heart of "great," which he articulated in a 1995 essay for *Inc.*, "Building Companies to Last: Embrace 'the Genius of the And.'"

A truly visionary company embraces both ends of a continuum: continuity *and* change, conservatism *and* progressiveness, stability *and* revolution, predictability *and* chaos, heritage *and* renewal, fundamentals *and* craziness. *And, and, and.*

For the most part, Collins seemed to call winners very well. A look at the companies he chose in relation to their Fortune 500 rankings in the decade that followed the publication of his book tells us that most of them held steady, having sustained the transition from good to great over the decade that followed their selection:

A Collins "Great"	*Fortune* 500 Ranking			
	2001	2005	2011	2012
Abbott Laboratories	144	100	71	70
Circuit City Stores (bankrupt in 2009)	155	231	--	--
Fannie Mae (involved in home mortgage scandal)	26	Not listed; House of Representatives approved overhaul in 2005	8	12
Gillette Company	188	215 Became a Procter & Gamble subsidiary in 2005	--	--
Kimberly-Clark	142	135	137	138
Kroger	18	21	23	23
Nucor	373	189	138	146
Philip Morris	Was an operating company of Altria until 2008		99	98
Pitney Bowes	379	392	461	489
Walgreens	90	38	32	37
Wells Fargo	62	52	26	25

Collins was exacting in his analysis, using a scientific process to narrow the number of companies from 1,435 to 11. He combined that process with the criterion that a company on the list had to demonstrate its good-to-great pattern of success independent of its industry; a booming company that was part of a similarly booming industry could not make the list.

Looking at the seven characteristics of companies that went from good to great through the lens of paradox, we might describe them as follows:

- **Level 5 Leadership.** The most successful leaders combine humility with confidence and determination, and these leaders can occur at every level. The interdependent pair they master is being _and_ doing.

- **First Who, Then What.** Collins suggests that recruiting the right people is the priority; after that, figure out what those people will do. This is a matter of balancing cultural fit _and_ performance fit. There is an implicit sense of overall direction, so leaders not only need to get the right people on board, but they also have to get the wrong people off the bus. Figuring out what those right people will do within the company may mean trying them out in different positions.

- **Confront the Brutal Facts.** Collins named this principle the Stockdale Paradox after Vice Admiral James Stockdale. In a conversation Collins had with him regarding his coping strategy as a prisoner of war in Vietnam, Stockdale said, "This is a very important lesson. You must never confuse faith that you will prevail in the end—which you can never afford to lose—with the discipline to confront the most brutal facts of your current reality, whatever they might be."[2] In other words, it's critical to accept your current reality _and_ create your future reality.

- **Hedgehog Concept.** The three overlapping considerations are passion, differentiation, and reward. In other words, you want to know what drives you, what distinguishes you, and what are people are willing to pay you. The first two are the paradox internal *and* external. The third embodies the paradox short term *and* long term.

▶ **Culture of Discipline** and **the Flywheel.** These two Collins principles belong together and as interdependent pair if you are viewing ideas through the lens of paradox. In a culture of discipline, adhering to a structure and systems that deliver consistent results is critical. It involves restraint. Referencing a practice of legendary triathlete Dave Scott, Collins calls this "rinsing the cottage cheese"—something that Scott did because he wanted to take every step possible to eliminate fat from his body. The Flywheel principle refers to the need to push, day after day, to achieve cumulative positive effects. If you keep pushing the wheel, it gains momentum; at that point, you've made a breakthrough. The Flywheel involves surplus—giving that extra bit every day to make sure the wheel keeps moving. So, the interdependent pair is restraint *and* surplus.

▶ **Technology Accelerators.** Using technology to accelerate growth means managing both people technology *and* process technology. People technology refers to using critical thinking skills (such as using paradox thinking!) and interpersonal skills to their fullest advantage. At the same time, there is an undeniable need for the technology support systems that process, store, and transmit data, and a host of other electronic and mechanical contributions to operations.

In the same book, Collins named what he called "comparators," meaning companies that had the same industry environment and opportunity to become great, but didn't achieve the growth Collins was looking for. Looking at these companies 10 years later, there are some insights to be gleaned that are salient in the discussion here about success stories. Just using the *Fortune* 500 rankings as an indicator, here is how comparators fared:

A Collins "Comparator"	*Fortune 500 Ranking*			
	2001	2005	2011	2012
Upjohn (brands and divisions sold to other companies)	--	--	--	--
Silo (went out of business in 1995	--	--	--	--
Great Western Bank (sold to another company)	--	--	--	--
Warner-Lambert (acquired in 2000)	--	--	--	--
Scott Paper (merged with Kimberly-Clark)	--	--	--	--
A&P (had a Fortune 500 ranking of 105 in 1995, and it was downhill from there; the company went bankrupt in 2010)	--	--	--	--
Bethlehem Steel (bankruptcy in 2001)	--	--	--	--
R. J. Reynolds	235	321	302	316
Addressograph (the name itself suggests the problem)	--	--	--	--
Eckerd (ranked 285 in 1997; the company was broken up and sold, with one of the buyers—CVS—gaining a giant footprint as a result)	--	--	--	--
Bank of America	13	18	13	21

The *Fortune* 500 ranking, which Collins valued as well in his initial selection criteria, is extremely useful because the companies on the list are sizable and publicly traded, so it's relatively easy to do a deep analysis of their practices and track record.

Analyzing Success (and Failure) With Paradox Thinking

I took a look at a couple of the same companies as Collins, as well as a classic "great" company—Boeing—using key paradoxes related to business strategy, core business process, corporate culture/shared values, and leadership. The paradoxes woven into the cases examined in the following two subsections include:

Business Strategy
- Logic *and* creativity.
- Short term *and* long term.
- Competition *and* cooperation.

Core Business Process
- Marketing *and* sales.
- Stability *and* change.
- Standardized *and* customized.

Corporate Culture/Shared Values
- Formal *and* informal.
- Plan-oriented *and* action-oriented.
- Traditional *and* innovative.

Leadership
- Leading *and* following.
- Directive *and* empowering.
- Strategic *and* tactical.

Analyzing Success (and Failure)

To begin, let's focus one of the several classic great companies that did not make the list. Companies such as GE, Coca-Cola, Disney, Intel, and Boeing were left off because, despite the fact that their earnings beat the market by 2.5 times in the 15-year period prior to publication of Collins's book, the good-to-greats outscored them threefold. Nonetheless, the classics have achieved perennial greatness due, in large part, to the balanced approach they take to key paradoxes such as those cited previously.

Boeing earned a 2012 rank of 30 on the *Fortune* 500 list, up from 39 in 2011. The largest aerospace company in the world secured its status thanks to a 1997 merger with McDonnell Douglas Corporation—my client at the time—and acquisition the previous year of Rockwell International's defense and space units. Timing may not be everything, but it certainly was important in these steps toward greatness.

Boeing wanted stability *and* change (that is, growth) as it headed into the new millennium. And, after rocky years in 1997–1998, Boeing achieved it. It acquired McDonnell Douglas after that company put its Total Quality Management (TQM) System in place and after the company sunk in value due in large part to defense contracts that were cancelled when the Cold War ended. As part of TQM, the company dramatically restructured and downsized its executive ranks: 5,200 managers, supervisors, and executives lost their jobs one miserable day in February 1989. They could reapply for the few thousand newly created jobs available, move into non-management positions, or leave. Those who reapplied went through a battery tests to determine their aptitude for leadership and team spirit. McDonnell Douglas had discovered the paradox that would enable them to cultivate bench strength. (McDonnell's CEO became president and COO of Boeing after the acquisition.) Two years later, after the Defense Department cancelled contracts related to the A-12 Avenger II program, McDonnell Douglas laid off another 5,600 employees. By the time Boeing bought the company in 1997, Boeing took over a lean, devalued operation with tremendous expertise and important resources. It set in motion steps for Boeing's next era of growth.

Pharmaceutical companies embody paradox because they are borne out of innovation, need to keep innovating to grow, yet face the persistent possibility that innovation will kill them. In other words, they need discoveries to exist, but it can be so difficult and expensive to bring those discoveries to market that their creative ambitions can doom them financially.

One of Collins's greats—and a former client of mine—is Abbott Laboratories. Founded in 1888, the company now serves more than 150 countries and has roughly 70,000 employees around the world contributing to its four core businesses in medical diagnostics, medical devices, nutrition, and pharmaceuticals. It ranks consistently among the top 100 companies on the *Fortune* 500 list.

Examined through the lens of paradox, Abbott Laboratories had the following successes. Two highlights follow:

Balancing Logic and Creativity

From its inception, Abbott Laboratories seems to have balanced logic and creativity in its business strategy. Founder Wallace Abbott, a practicing physician who also owned a drug store, recognized that the administering of medicines involved a little too much guesswork. He invented the use of pills—consistent dosages of medication— by taking the active part of medicinal plants and forming them into "dosimetric granules." As a corollary, his invention didn't remove the creative aspects of care giving; it made it easier for clinicians to focus on them.

Any company that wants to succeed long-term in the arenas of pharmaceuticals and health care products would have to learn to keep logic and creativity working together toward the Aim. Abbott's tagline, "Turning science into caring," sets up the paradox of logic and creativity that is evident throughout descriptions of the company's four businesses. Concepts such as accuracy, efficiency, and consistency are therefore paired with "new formulations" and "innovative delivery methods."

Focusing on Both Stability and Change

Many aspects of the company, principally corporate values, have remained stable through the years. Its various acquisitions and divestitures are one indicator that it also changes to operate more effectively and profitability in the context of its industry and the context of the markets in which it operates. In January 2013, the company also effected a significant change: Abbott split into two publicly-traded companies. One is comprised of four equal-sized businesses: nutritionals, diagnostics, devices, and generic pharmaceuticals. The other, called AbbVie, is a research-based biopharmaceutical company that includes Abbott's portfolio of proprietary pharmaceuticals and biologics.

———

Companies in the industry that made Collins's comparator list morphed and merged and ultimately, a few phoenix arose from the ashes (flapping at least one wing). Rather than do a one-on-one look at those companies—the model for the subsequent discussion of two major manufacturing companies—let's focus on a few insights about the success (and failure) factors for any pharmaceutical industry player. The role of managing paradoxes in surviving and thriving is the theme of various critiques from analysts.

In *Forbes*, analyst Christopher Bowe noted: "To save itself—and save more patients—the industry should take two vital steps: develop a more flexible approach to drug approval and patent exclusivity and change its business model to encourage more scientific collaboration among companies. The first change is relatively closer to our grasp; the second requires a sea change in the industry."[3]

In terms of a key business strategy paradox, Bowe's comment addresses the way companies create and manage their competitive advantage and the way they partner with competitors—that is, competition *and* cooperation.

Dana Radcliff, Day Family senior lecturer in business ethics at Cornell University, looked at the disastrous irony of pharmaceutical companies managing a paradox supporting a negative Aim to help them thrive—at least until they got caught. It might be best summarized as empowering physicians *and* controlling physicians. In his article, he spotlights GlaxoSmithKline's $3 billion fine, paid in July 2012 to resolve civil and criminal liabilities regarding its promotion of drugs. It's only fair to note, however, that eight other major companies in the industry—including Abbott—also paid hefty fines between January 2009 and December 2012 for comparable or identical tactics.

Glaxo intentionally conflicted physicians, giving them incentives to make prescription decisions based on their own interests rather than what was best for their patients. Thus, Glaxo profited by undermining the doctors' autonomy—their capacity to make professionally sound, unbiased decisions. At the same time, company executives could allay any ethical concerns by convincing themselves that the conflicted doctors exercised complete autonomy in writing prescriptions, which would absolve Glaxo of any responsibility for the consequences.[4]

Radcliff continued his analysis with an explanation of what might drive a good company to even consider supporting a negative Aim— profit at all costs—like the one he features. The powerful answer is "context."

Assuming Glaxo executives are not wicked people who don't care if their actions endanger others, then it must be that they saw nothing wrong with the aggressive measures Glaxo took in trying to reach its sales targets. No doubt this is partly due to the fact that, in the late 1990s and early 2000s (when much of the misconduct occurred), its main competitors relied on the same marketing tactics, so that such things as promoting off-label uses and incentivizing doctors were industry norms.[5]

The takeaway message is that political, economic, social, and technical/operations factors all shape the environment in which a company operates, but it is possible to have that context be severely distorted by excessive influence of one or two over the others. The early-2000s scandals of the pharmaceutical industry, mid-2000s financial services crisis, and similar blights in the world of business rose out of such lack of balance.

Analyzing Failure (and Success)

When the *Fortune* 500 list premiered in 1955, Bethlehem Steel was ranked number 8. It had been a powerhouse throughout World War II, and is credited with building 1,127 ships during the war as well as serving as the steel supplier for the bridges and tunnels used by anyone who commutes between New Jersey and Manhattan. As the years went by, Bethlehem Steel kept slipping in rank on the list. Starting in 1977, it had year after year of significant losses.

Examined through the lens of paradox, Bethlehem Steel made the following errors.

Short Term at the Neglect of Long Term

If you had quizzed a Bethlehem Steel executive in the early 1970s about short-term focus, at least in some instances, he would have argued that you got it backward—that the company had its eye on the long-term implications of its investments. The prime example is the company's heavy investments in plant upgrades. But look closely at where a big portion of the cash should have gone and the neglect of long term becomes clear. Bethlehem Steel had enormous commitments to pension plans for its unionized workforce, but failed to make yearly contributions to the pension fund, instead choosing to do infrastructure improvements. When the demand for domestic steel plunged and the company had to close plants and lay off workers, revenue started to dry up, but the pension obligations remained. By the mid-1980s, after going from employing about 167,000 people in the mid-1950s to a work-force of 35,000, Bethlehem Steel actually had twice as many retirees and dependents to support as they did workers: that is, 70,000 people. By the time the company declared bankruptcy in 2001, the company employed 11,500 people and had ongoing obligations to an additional 120,000 retirees and their dependents. The company issued letters asking for patience to those retirees, such as one about health benefits, dated October 31, 2002 that began:

Dear Member of the Bethlehem Health Care Family:

This past year has been the most difficult time in our company's nearly 100-year history. Bethlehem's strong commitment to survive and prosper is contingent upon addressing the $3 billion retiree welfare benefits legacy costs. Without significant changes to our retiree health and life insurance obligations, we cannot successfully restructure and emerge from bankruptcy.[6]

This was followed by a March 25, 2003 letter to retirees and dependents on that conveyed a decidedly less hopeful message. Making no mention of a Bethlehem "Family," it began:

Dear Bethlehem Steel Retiree:

On March 24, 2003, the U.S. Bankruptcy Court, having jurisdiction of Bethlehem's bankruptcy cases, authorized Bethlehem to terminate the retiree medical and life insurance benefits for essentially all of its retirees, surviving spouses and eligible dependents effective March 31, 2003. This means that Bethlehem will no longer pay any claim for retiree medical services incurred after March 31, 2003.[7]

In contrast, Bethlehem Steel's prime competitor, United States Steel, funded its pension and benefits plans regularly and aggressively. At the same time, U.S. Steel made some valuable non-steel acquisitions, such as Marathon Oil, which it later spun off—so it did have its eye on both short-term and long-term considerations. Most recently, its investments in plant upgrades related to software upgrades. As of 2012, it was still a *Fortune 500* company, ranked at 147.

Stability at the Neglect of Change

U.S. Steel plunged into diversification when the steel market weakened dramatically in the early 1980s. It never abandoned its core business, but its foray into the oil business, for example, helped to even its cash flow. In contrast, Bethlehem Steel remained a steel company.

Formal *and* Informal, but Contrasting for Executives and Workers

The cultural tension at Bethlehem Steel was a problem of bifurcation more than a problem of either formal or informal. Executives had their formal culture, as well as an informal one where, for many years, it was practically a requirement that executives play golf. Workers had their formal culture, as defined by the United Steelworkers of America, as well as a palpable informal culture. Anyone old enough to remember what it was like to grow up in a "steel town" during years when steel was the king of metals in the United States knows that the informal culture of steelworkers involved feelings of pride and strength. Anyone who grew up in a "steel town" beginning in the 1970s experienced the aftermath of both the formal and informal cultures of steelworkers imploding. The paradox that the company did not manage, therefore, might best be captured as formal and informal executive culture *and* formal and informal worker culture.

Plan-Oriented at the Neglect of Action-Oriented

The company held tenaciously to certain plans that cost them dearly. One of them was the pension and healthcare benefits plans for employees. Although that plan could be construed as reflecting concern for employees, company executives low-balled the costs and never took action to adjust the plans or face the reality of the costs.

Leading at the Neglect of Following

Going back to the longtime legendary—and because of his war efforts, even heroic—leadership of Eugene Gifford Grace, Bethlehem Steel was known for leaders who dug in their heels and "dug their hole deeper," in the words of *Fortune* reporter Carol J. Loomis, who wrote an "autopsy" of the former steel giant in April 2004.[8] Grace was famous for having the minions ensure he rode the elevator to his posh office alone.

Directive at the Neglect of Empowering

In 2003, International Steel Group (ISG) began operating six of Bethlehem Steel's plants. The contract ISG negotiated flattened the relationships between workers quite a bit, and made management and workers more of a team. This was not a model that Bethlehem Steel embraced or ever even experimented with. There was no concept of team; at the same time, there was an inordinate investment in the people who espoused "directive" at the neglect of "empowering." At ISG, there were three layers of management between the CEO, Wilbur Ross, and the steelworkers. At Bethlehem Steel, there were eight—eight layers of people directing.

———

To quantify the failures of Bethlehem Steel's executives in managing key paradoxes, we can turn to the chilling summary that Loomis did of the company's track record of return on equity.

The fact is that for 16 years, beginning in 1958, Bethlehem never came close to the 500's return on equity (ROE), which for those years averaged 11.2 percent. Bethlehem consistently did no better than a single-digit return and sank down to 4.6 percent one year. Overall, its ROE averaged a mere 7.5 percent, almost four percentage points less than that of the 500. That's a huge inferiority, signaling a company that was in deep trouble. Grown-up businesses generating ROEs like that are the kind that investors want to run from, as fast as possible.[9]

Case Study Wrap-Up

The previous discussions of Affirm Health described 12 key paradoxes with half of them falling thematically into the category of "control and freedom." The interrelated issues in this grouping are:

Tight systems *and* flexibility in care.

Master plan *and* responsiveness to needs.

Headquarters perspective *and* hospital perspective.

Company standard *and* market brand.

Centralized control *and* distributed leadership.

Nurturing relationship with managers/leaders *and* asserting expertise.

It makes sense, then, in taking actions to achieve an Aim of "growth," which can be seen as both revenue growth and service growth, that the organization would focus a great deal of attention on the "control and freedom" paradoxes.

The challenge is that Affirm has been decentralized because of the way it has grown. As of 2013, it had a presence in nearly half of the United States with massive growth occurring through acquisitions. The Affirm system, therefore, represents a conglomeration of different cultures and contexts. Given this situation, leadership recognized that, to provide the best care, the components of the organization needed to come together in more ways as a unified system. And Affirm needed to make some major revisions in operations so it could make sound, data-driven decisions.

There was a sense of urgency linked to the changes in U.S. health-care laws[10] that would most likely affect their level of reimbursements. Across-the-board efficiency upgrades would be the only way to maintain and improve standards of care in the face of diminishing income from some key sources. By being too heavily focused on a distributed model, they couldn't rein in costs. Affirm's shared services initiative, begun in 2012, illustrates one way the organization hopes to succeed in managing a few key paradoxes, one outcome of which would be to reduce costs by eliminating redundancy of certain services by centralizing them. This is part of their strategy to take a highly distributed model and balance operations with selected centralized processes, fostering cooperation across individual business units. To effect a rapid transition to shared services, Affirm's leadership brought in a global consulting firm, which helped the organization get the initiative up and running in only 18 months.

Affirm took a giant step in creating a shared services group at the corporate level. The facilities didn't lose their individual, local identity or the kind of autonomy that's vital to patient care, but rather they gained efficiency through shared resources. The new system is a definite move to leverage the upsides of both decentralized and centralized.

There is always caution when moving to a more centralized business model. You could swing the pendulum too far, but it seems unlikely at this point due to the checks and balances already in place and as part of the ramp-up to implementing this initiative.

Case in point: The Facilities Task Force, referenced in earlier chapters, is critical in reinforcing the balance between clinical and facilities needs. Launched in 2010, one of the actions the Task Force took was creating an Infrastructure Investment Fund. Each year, Affirm allocates between up to $50 million for facilities projects across the system that have been nominated for funding. They are evaluated based on factors such as life-safety risk and energy efficiency. The Task Force director has noted how the Fund reflects a focus on both clinical needs *and* facilities needs. Specifically, facilities projects are no longer competing against MRI machines or other health or clinical needs. Instead facility managers alert the Task Force to projects where failures could occur and would negatively affect the hospitals' care of patients.

Companies with a focus on organic growth—that is, growth through expansion of existing divisions and business units—also have to balance issues of autonomy with those of corporate dictates. However, through practices such as promoting from within, it is easier to cultivate a shared culture with a common focus than in an organization like Affirm.

Affirm's growth-through-acquisitions strategy gives rise to more complex issues related to culture and context. The great success of an organization like Affirm is the commitment of leadership at various levels to achieve greater alignment by balancing seemingly conflicting needs, points of view, and options. This commitment has led to innovative solutions that effectively address their mission *and* margin challenges.

As complexity grows, so does the need for paradox thinking.

Conclusion

On the first page in this book, I started building the case that "and" thinking breaks through barriers to problem solving and innovation. Yes, you can have a muscle car that gets good gas mileage. Yes, you should be both logical and emotional about your health. Yes, you can have an organization that provides customized, local service at the same time it's a centralized, global company.

The implications of embracing such paradoxes for organizations, leaders, and all of us on a day-to-day basis are profound. For organizational success, doing so is also absolutely necessary.

Why?

Futurist Joel Barker set the stage for the answer to this question when he said, "When paradigms shift, everyone goes back to zero!"[1] Players change, the game changes, and the rules of the game change.

Leaders at all levels of business need to recognize that the paradigms are shifting. They need to heed the caution issued by McKinsey & Company in an October 2013 white paper called "Urban World: The Shifting Global Business Landscape": "Business leaders need a better understanding of the current corporate landscape and how it is evolving in order to anticipate where the global economy is headed and how to prepare for a new wave of competitors."[2] The study describes the evolution in terms of numbers of large companies, revenues and locations of those companies, and corporate ownership. Among other things, it predicts a dramatic shift upward in the number of companies exceeding the large-company benchmark of $1 billion in annual revenues and a dramatic shift downward in the number of large companies that are located in developed regions of the world. In short, by 2025 we should see about 15,000 companies with more than $1 billion in annual revenue spread out all over the world, with a great many new ones located in China. These numbers are one type of evidence that the players are changing, the game is changing, and the rules of the game are changing.

The McKinsey team points to three key imperatives for businesses to heed in order to survive and thrive in the new landscape—and there is at least one significant paradox inherent in each one:

1. **Optimize sales network according to where business customers are based.** Businesses will need to organize themselves to reach a more diverse and dispersed customer base *and* to remain attentive and responsive to their existing customers.

2. **Understand how the ecosystem for customers and competitors is evolving.** Business leaders need to watch for new sources of innovation with their focus currently on potentially disruptive change as it relates to their customers and competitors *and* change with explosive potential as it pertains to them. A related, simple paradox is the balance of focus on customers *and* competitors.

3. **Reconsider headquarters configuration and location choices.** The paradox in this is akin to the Three Musketeers' slogan: "All for one and one for all." A single-headquarters model may not make sense for some global businesses. Yet, even if there are multiple headquarters so that main offices align with key markets, all locations still are part of one company and supporting common Aims.

Running through the entire discussion of the new business landscape, but not specifically articulated in the McKinsey report, is the importance of companies staying focused on global *and* local. Even small companies have the ability to leverage Web-based resources to establish a global presence, so the interdependent pair no longer applies to giant corporations with a physical presence in multiple countries. This is the kind of paradigm shift that Barker was referring to his remark that "everyone goes back to zero."

Another example of such a shift, which is also related to electronic connectivity, is the rise of innovative businesses involving huge numbers of contributors from around the world. Wikipedia is a successful non-profit pioneer with this model; Quirky is a successful for-profit pioneer. Founded in 2001, Wikipedia now has more than 70,000 active contributors working on more than 22,000,000 articles in 285 languages. Quirky is a New York–based company that encompasses a growing community of 500,000 users who evaluate ideas for new inventions and then collaboratively make them happen. For example, the company notes that Jake Zien and 853 other people invented a product called Pivot Power. The contributors are not volunteers, either: They are getting paid for expertise such as research, design, sales, tag lines, and more.

The success of these companies spotlights one of the key paradoxes—in fact, a pervasive quandary—for many organizations founded prior to the World Wide Web: the balance of physical *and* digital. These companies were not "born" with both factors present in their business model, so their significant paradigm shift is transforming that model to acknowledge the importance of the interdependent pair.

For example, museums may have curators and historians who find the notion of a virtual museum tour appalling. Similarly, professors in any subject may find online courses an affront to quality education. And companies may struggle with the customer-interaction challenges related to online retail sites. But the Web is ubiquitous in any modern society, so it makes no business sense to ignore digital and focus solely on physical. As a corollary, those organizations that require a physical presence—like museums, most universities, and stores that have established themselves as a "destination location"—erode their brand-ing if they over-focus on building their digital presence.

Senior leaders of such organizations need to start the shift toward managing the paradox by having teams that embrace the Aim. Any-thing short of that—such as a slight variation on the Aim—suggests that the effort will be doomed to fail, with an over-focus on one part of the pair at the neglect of the other.

In the case of one prominent New York art museum, "physical" has always represented their approach to achieving "mission"—that is, to give visitors personal exposure to authentic examples of fine art. With the proliferation of computing devices, the museum has many opportunities to bring its education-based value to a broader global audience in addition to the traditional visit to their physical locations. In a sense, then, "digital" represents a significant new way to achieve "margin." Their paradox, therefore, is to maintain their mission focus while also developing revenue streams reflecting the possibilities tech-nology provides. The challenge is analogous to the one that private museums with an entrance fee face in Washington, DC, where the vast and varied holdings of the Smithsonian Institution are freely accessible to the public.

The museum is succeeding because everyone on board has an eye on the mission of being the best museum of its kind in the world. My colleague Jon Wheeler has used the tools of paradox thinking described throughout this book to illuminate how both physical and digital are necessary—not just "great to have" but _necessary_—in achieving that Aim. He has been helping the museum find ways to think and operate more with a strategic and tactical focus on both of the interdependent opposites.

What if leaders at all levels in organizations identified vital oppor-tunities to use paradox thinking? We would start to see more balance in strategy and tactics designed to achieve the Aim. We would have less idiosyncratic and/or cavalier decision-making. We would have fewer disasters borne out of the misplaced use of either/or thinking.

The previous chapters opened with quotes that captured themes running throughout the chapters. Here, I will move toward a close with insights that capture prime themes running throughout the book. They are from Douglas Conant, retired CEO of Campbell Soup Company and author of *Touchpoints*. In an interview with leadership consultant and award-winning blogger Dan Rockwell (aka "The Leadership Freak"), Conant told him that moving from "or" thinking to "and" thinking most changed his leadership. He then hit on the points that create a-ha moments for my clients—the thoughts that propel them into the immense power of paradox thinking:[3]

▶ "And" thinking embraces abundance thinking.

▶ "And" takes you further than "or." "Or" thinking limits your potential by creating artificial barriers to creativity, excellence, and diversity. "And" thinking creates challenges, opportunities, and innovation.

When you begin to think in terms of "and," you have a whole new world of answers to who, what, when, where, why, and how when it comes to your success. You have a powerful tool for illuminating various perspectives on key issues to solve problems and achieve your goals. You can harness the energy of competing ideas to uncover radically innovative solutions.

Appendix

How-to Summary

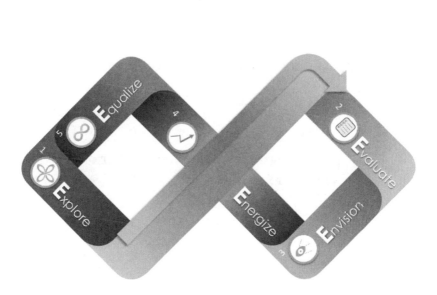

The macro steps captured in this graphic are a guide to the exercises woven through Part I and Part II of the book.

1. Explore the types of paradoxes that your organization faces. See Chapter 3.

   ▶ Throw all the issues on the table.

   ▶ Put them into pairs of conflicting needs.

   ▶ Group those pairs thematically.

2. Evaluate when paradox thinking is necessary and when it's important to see choices as either one or another. See Chapter 3.

   ▶ When paradox thinking is necessary:

      • When you are working through complex situations and complex relationships.

      • When both "needs" are critical for achieving your Aim.

      • When problems are ongoing and there is appears to be an interdependency.

      • *Note: The types of questions that involve paradox thinking are why and how questions.*

   ▶ When applying either/or thinking is necessary:

      • When the situation is urgent—a life or death situation.

      • When it is impossible to choose both "alternatives"; they are discrete.

   Note: The types of questions that involve either/or thinking are who, what, when, and where questions.

3. Envision the Aim, the Miss, and the possible positive and negative outcomes for your organization when you focus on each need separately and then together. See Chapter 5.

   ▶ Draw an infinity loop on a white board or a flip chart.

   ▶ Write the conflicting needs in the infinity loop, one on the left, one on the right.

   ▶ Brainstorm the positive and negative outcomes for each competing need. Note: Negative outcomes surface as a result of over-focus on one need at the neglect of the other.

4. Energize the solution: Move out of the analysis stages and into actionable implementation to manage and leverage your paradoxes. See Chapter 6.

   ◗ Focusing on the left side of your model, determine the actions that are necessary to achieve the stated positive outcomes

   ◗ Focusing on the right side of your model, determine the actions that are necessary to achieve the stated positive outcomes

   ◗ Once actions have been generated, reflect on the following questions.

     • What action steps should we take to get these positive outcomes?

     • How does the proposed action step correlate to a specified need?

     • Is there more than one way to do that?

     • Does the action reflect what we know about the business environment?

     • What do you know about the business environment that would accelerate positive results from the action and what do you know that would inhibit positive results?

5. Equalize the execution; that is, put qualitative and quantitative measures in place to help indicate risk as you gauge progress. See Chapter 7.

   ◗ Focusing on the left side of your model, determine the indicators that would signal when negative outcomes are beginning to surface.

   ◗ Focusing on the right side of your model, determine the indicators that would signal when negative outcomes are beginning to surface.

   ◗ Once identified, zero in on the key measures, keeping in mind industry-specific tools.

Visualize how these steps are connected and flow from one to the other, with the process repeating again and again. The steps have an energetic relationship. When practiced over time, this thinking becomes fluid and brings value instantly to your work life and your whole life.

Notes

Author's Notes

1. Russell L. Ackoff (1973), "Science in the Systems Age: Beyond IE, OR and MS," *Operations Research* Vol. 21, pp. 664.

2. *www.polaritypartnerships.com.* My exposure to Barry Johnson began in 2002, working together with him on a client project. My learning deepened with further study in a two-part Consultant Development Intensive and two-year mastery program focused on polarity.

Introduction

1. *http://editorial.autos.msn.com/new-cars-muscle-versus-mileage?icid=autos_4563.*

2. Ibid.

3. Trevor Crow and Maryann Karinch, *Forging Healthy Relationships,* New Horizon Press, 2013, p. 5.

4. John Kenneth Galbraith, *Economics, Peace and Laughter,* 1971, p. 50.

Chapter 1

1. George Bernard Shaw, *Maxims for Revolutionists,* 1903, 124.

Chapter 2

1. Fons Trompenaars and Charles Hampden-Turner, *Riding the Waves of Culture, Third Edition*, McGraw-Hill, 2011.

2. Ibid, p. 85.

3. Dean Hohl and Maryann Karinch, *Rangers Lead the* Way, Adams Media, 2003, pp. 154–155.

Chapter 3

1. Michael E. Raynor and Mumtaz Ahmed, "Three Rules for Making a Company Truly Great" *Harvard Business Review*, April 2013, pp. 108–117.

2. Mike Brown, "Acer to Stop Making 'Cheap and Unprofitable Products,'" Neowin.net, *www.neowin.net/news/acer-to-stop-making-cheap-and-unprofitable-products*.

3. Raynor and Ahmed, op. cit.

4. Dominic Dodd and Ken Favaro, *The Three Tensions: Winning the Struggle to Perform Without Compromise*, Jossey-Bass, 2007.

5. Ibid.

Chapter 4

1. *www.kotterinternational.com/our-principles/changesteps/changesteps*.

2. Ibid.

3. Robert W. Jacobs, "Practical Guide to Real Time Strategic Change," based on material in *Real-Time Strategic Change: How to Involve an Entire Organization in Fast and Far-Reaching Change*, Berrett-Koehler, 1997.

4. Tariq K. Muhammad, "On Top of the World," *Black Enterprise*, June 1999, *www.blackenterprise.com/mag/on-top-of-the-world/*.

5. Ibid.

6. *www2.wwt.com/content/executive-team*.

7. *www.ssmhc.com/internet/home/ssmcorp. nsf/57fcb4c601b6208e862573e200544abb/ fa639433854c987a862573cc0059fd16?OpenDocument*.

8. Personal conversation, October 15, 2013.

Chapter 5

1. For more on the important of this see the article by Burkard Polster, "Juggle, Maths, and a Beautiful Mind," *http://plus.maths. org/content/juggling-maths-and-beautiful-mind*.

Chapter 6

1. Fred Reichheld and Rob Markey, "Winning Results With NPS: Ten Net Promoter Success Stories; How Forward-Thinking Companies Thrive in a Customer-Driven World," *The Harvard Business Review*, 2011, pp. 8–9.

2. Jonathan D. Glater, "Law Firms Feel Strain of Layoffs and Cutbacks, *The New York Times*, November 11, 2008.

3. *http://lawshucks.com/layoff-tracker/*.

4. "Leading Christian Charity IBS-STL UK Announces Plans to Sell Operations Due to Financial Challenges," *http://stldistribution. blogspot.com/2009/11/ibs-stl-uk-trade-communication. html?showComment=1258403900001*.

Chapter 7

1. Personal conversation, April 19, 2013.

Chapter 8

1. Ackoff, op. cit.

2. Jason Nolte, "Why Americans Hate Sears," MSN Money, *http:// money.msn.com/now/post.aspx?post=32a6436c-c2c2-46f5-b52d-102f17f26d37*.

3. Rupal Parekh, "Kmart Continues the Puns With its 'Big Gas' Promotion," *Ad Age*, May 23, 2013.

4. *http://ameren.mediaroom.com/index.php?s=43&item=1129*.

5. Jessi Hempel, "LinkedIn: How It's Changing Business (and How to Make it Work for You," *Fortune*, July 1, 2013, p. 70.

6. Ibid, p. 72.

7. From Wikipedia: Edward Joseph "Ed" Snowden is an American computer specialist and a former CIA and NSA employee

who has leaked details of several top-secret United States and British government mass surveillance programs to the press. Based on information Snowden leaked to *The Guardian* in May 2013 while employed at NSA contractor Booz Allen Hamilton, the British newspaper published a series of exposés that revealed programs such as the interception of U.S. and European telephone metadata and the PRISM, XKeyscore, and Tempora Internet surveillance programs.

8. Cheryl Conner, "The Good, The Bad and The Tragic: Stories of Acquisition for Growth," *Forbes*, March 17, 2013, *www.forbes.com/sites/cherylsnappconner/2013/03/17/the-good-the-bad-and-the-tragic-stories-of-acquisition-for-growth/*.

9. Anne Law, "IPC the Hospitalist Company, Inc.—Quick Report," Hoover's, March 6, 2013.

10. *http://medical-dictionary.thefreedictionary.com/hospitalist*.

11. Anne Law, op. cit.

Chapter 10

1. Jim Collins, *Good to Great*, HarperBusiness, 2001, p. 6.

2. Ibid., p. 13.

3. Christopher Bowe, "Big Pharma Failures Light the Way to Change," *Forbes*, August 16, 2012, *www.forbes.com/sites/matthewherper/2012/08/16/big-pharma-failures-light-the-way-to-change/*.

4. Dana Radcliff, "A Drug-Maker's Ethical 'Mistakes'," *Huffington Post*, August 6, 2012, *www.huffingtonpost.com/dana-radcliffe/a-drugmakers-ethical-mist_b_1729002.html*.

5. Ibid.

6. From a letter archived by Ann M. Karinch, one of the 120,000-plus Bethlehem Steel dependents entitled to benefits at the time of the company's bankruptcy.

7. Ibid.

8. Carol J. Loomis, "The Sinking of Bethlehem Steel," *Fortune*, April 5, 2004.

9. Ibid.

10. From Wikipedia: "The Patient Protection and Affordable Care Act (PPACA),[1] commonly called the Affordable Care Act (ACA) or Obamacare,[2][3] is a United States federal statute signed into law by President Barack Obama on March 23, 2010. Together with the Health Care and Education Reconciliation Act,[4] it represents the most significant regulatory overhaul of the country's healthcare system since the passage of Medicare and Medicaid in 1965." *http://en.wikipedia.org/wiki/Patient_Protection_and_Affordable_Care_Act*.

Conclusion

1. *www.innovationprocess.co/when-paradigms-shift-everyone-goes-back-to-zero/*.

2. Richard Dobbs, Jaana Remes, Sven Smit, James Manyika, Jonathan Woetzel, and Yaw Agyenim-Boateng, "Urban World: The Shifting Global Business Landscape," McKinsey Global Institute, McKinsey & Company, October 13, Executive Summary.

3. *http://leadershipfreak.wordpress.com/2011/08/23/a-ceo-of-campbells-explains-the-power-of-and/*.

Index

A

Abbott Laboratories, 215, 221-223

Acritas, 154

action plan, 140, 176-177, 199

Affirm Health, 36-39, 52-53, 79-83, 86, 143-146, 228-231

Ameren Corporation, 182

B

becoming a leader, 114-119

Bethlehem Steel, 224-228

Boeing, 219-221

both/and as a complement to either/or, 91-94

business cycle stage
  established, 67-68
  exit, 70
  expansion, 68-69
  growth, 67
  incubator, 66
  mature, 69-70
  startup, 67

business strategy. 49-50, 59, 118, 219, 221, 223

C

categories of paradox, 49

changing leadership, 100-103

chronic struggle, 75-76

complex paradox, 45

context, 179-186

core business , 40, 51, 109,
130-133, 182, 219, 226
process, 51

corporate culture, 51-53, 92, 118,
166, 219

Culture of Disciple, 217

E

Eastman Kodak, 179-181

either/or in planning, 88-91

ENERGY STAR program, 96

established stage, 67-68

evaluating when paradox thinking
is necessary, 85-88, 94-97

exit stage, 70

expansion stage, 68

F

fear response, 101

fears and values, paradoxes that
reflect, 74-75

Flywheel, 217

Ford Motor Company, 169-171

Fortune 100, 185

Fortune 500, 214-221, 224, 226

from-to relationships, 76-79

G

Glaxo, 223

global business trends, 63-66

global culture, 54-55

growth stage, 67

GT Bicycles, 153

H

Hedgehog Concept, 216-217

HomeAway, 188

Hostess Brands, 148-152

I

identifying paradoxes in your organization, 82-84

incubator stage, 66

Internet Engineering Task Force (IETF), 187

IPC–The Hospitalist Company, 173-176, 188-189, 192-194

ITHRes. 39, 50, 74, 90-91, 134, 137

K

Kmart, 180

L

leading
    people, 55-57
    teams, 57-58

Lehman Brothers, 156-157

Levy's Management Philosophy and Leadership Principles, 113

linear thinker, 24-25

LinkedIn, 184-186

Livli Hotels, 32-35, 44, 50, 76-79, 88-89, 207-210

M

Maslow's Hierarchy, 100

mature stage, 69-70

McDonnell Douglas, 220, 237

MetLife, 27, 164

metrics undermining success, 168-171

N

Nash, John Forbes Jr., 123-125

nature/nurture paradox, 59-63

nested paradoxes, 45-46

Net Promoter, 146-148, 173

O

organizational change process strategy, 104-107

P

paradox, categories of, 49

paradox, definition of, 24-25

paradoxes in your organization, identifying, 82-84

Paraquad, 199-201

pulling themes from a conversation, 79-81

Q

Quaker Oats, 186

Questor Partners Fund, 153

R

Reinsurance Group of America (RGA), 27, 56, 112, 164-165, 168

restructuring/merging/acquisition paradox, 59

Rubin's vase, 123-124

S

Schwinn Bicycles, 152-154

Scottrade, 156-157

Sears, 180-181

Send the Light, 157-158

shared paradoxes, 70-71

shared values, 51-53, 202, 219

Shrades, 202-206

simple paradox, 45

Snapple Beverage Company, 186

SoCA Real Estate, 130-133

SSM Health Care–St. Louis, 110-112

St. Louis Finance, 29-30, 32, 51, 128, 137

stacked paradoxes, 47-48

startup stage, 67

sustainability, 15, 37, 108, 112, 130-133, 156, 158, 172, 213-214

sylibrium, 31

T

talent/staff/people paradox, 59

Technology Accelerators, 217

Total Quality Management (TQM) System, 220

U

using metrics, 173-177

W

World Wide Technology, 108-109

Y

Yankee Candle, 109-110

About the Author

DEBORAH SCHROEDER-SAULNIER, D.Mgt., president and CEO of Excel Leadership Solutions, is a highly sought advisor to senior executives. Leveraging her 25-year career in senior leadership roles, and consulting to business/industry, she partners closely with executives to solve problems, clarify focus, and accelerate the pursuit of critical market, organization, and leadership priorities. She has worked with a number of Fortune 500 companies worldwide, including Boeing, Citigroup, Bunge LTD., Scottrade, Danfoss, Georgia-Pacific, IPC-The Hospitalist Company, RGA—Reinsurance Group of America, and World Wide Technology. Her company Website is *www.excelleadershipsolutions.com*. She is based in St. Louis, Missouri.